THE
ALL-AGE
SERVICE
ANNUAL

VOLUME TWO

15 Bible-based service outlines for those
who plan or lead All-Age Worship

Copyright © Scripture Union 2008

ISBN 978 1 84427 341 5

Scripture Union, 207–209 Queensway, Bletchley, MK2 2EB, England.
Email: info@scriptureunion.org.uk
Website: www.scriptureunion.org.uk

Scripture Union Australia
Locked Bag 2, Central coast Business Centre, NSW 2252, Australia
Website: www.scriptureunion.org.au

Scripture Union USA,
PO Box 987, Valley Forge, PA 19482, USA
Website: www.scriptureunion.org

British Library Cataloguing-in-Publication Data
A catalogue record for this book is available from the British Library.

Printed by Tien Wah Press, Malaysia
Cover design iedesign
Internal layout Helen Jones

Scripture Union is an international Christian charity working with churches in more
than 130 countries, providing resources to bring the good news about Jesus to children, young people and
families and encourage them to develop spiritually through the Bible and prayer.

As well as our network of volunteers, staff and associates who run holidays, church-based events and school
Christian groups, we produce a wide range of publications and support those who use our resources
through training programmes.

Contents

Welcome! to this volume of the *All-Age Service Annual*, the resource that takes the stress out of planning and leading all-age services.

In this volume you will find 15 creative outlines to be used throughout the year. They cover all the major festivals as well as providing you with two series of outlines on Elisha and Matthew. The series could be used in the order printed in this book, consecutively in regular services or over a holiday period. For example, some churches disband their regular children's and youth programmes over the summer and run a series of all-age services instead. Every service is Bible-based and provides readings from both the Old and New Testaments.

Your children's or youth groups may use resources from Scripture Union's *Light* curriculum material. If so, each outline is linked to one month's *Light* theme during the 2008/9 year– see the *Light Link*. This means that what the children and young people are learning in their groups could be reinforced or introduced in the all-age service. All these outlines, however, work effectively with no reference to *Light*.

Other Scripture Union all-age resources :

All-Age Service Starters
In many services children and young people may join in for just part of the service. To cater for this, the All-Age Service Starters are available, for free, as downloads from www.scriptureunion.org.uk/light. These provide four suggestions for activities connected to the relevant *Light* theme to be used in the part of a service when all ages are present.

Light for the Lectionary
Light for the Lectionary is published quarterly. It contains 15 flexible all-age service outlines that develop Bible passages and themes from the *Revised Common Lectionary* and *Common Worship*. For more details visit www.scriptureunion.org.uk/light.

Top Tips on All-age worship
This is a 32-page book full of practical pointers on working with children and young people to help you reflect on and evaluate your all-age services. Other particularly useful Top Tips titles are *Growing faith with families* and *Encouraging faith to grow*.

The All-Age Service Annual was developed in direct response to research carried out by Scripture Union into the practices and needs of churches with regard to all-age worship. We received feedback on Volume 1, of which we have taken heed and so the format of Volume 2 has been amended. We hope that as you read and use these outlines with your congregation you will feel that they meet your needs and enable your church family to encounter the living God in your worship together. We welcome all feedback from those who use our material so please let us know any comments and suggestions that you have.

Ro Willoughby
Editor

We would like to thank the following for their writing contributions:
Piers Lane, Robert Willoughby, Ruth Wills, John Grayston, Jack Bull, Andy Gray, Sarah Bingham, Alex Taylor, Brad Lincoln, Rachel Taylor, Helen Jones, Darren Hill and 'Tricia Williams

Using the All-Age Service Annual

Leading worship is both a great privilege and a great responsibility. Many people leading all-age services would say that they often take far more time to prepare than other services, especially if other people are involved and the service is going to be interactive, using props, crafts and drama. So allow sufficient time to prepare for your service.

Every service outline in the *All-Age Service Annual* is made up of the following components:

Background	**Praise**
Light **Link**	**Prayers of intercession**
Introduction	**Response**
Prayers of confession	**Prayers of thanksgiving**
Reading the Bible	**God's blessing**
Bible talk	

With the exception of the first three, these components will be arranged in a different order for different services (though note that 'God's blessing' will normally appear as the last item). You may need to rearrange the order according to what will work best with your congregation. Similarly, you may want to amend or leave out altogether any components which, in your opinion, might hinder rather than help everyone in their all-age worship. We would strongly recommend, however, that you always include the public reading of the Bible.

Make sure you adapt the language in the *All-Age Service Annual* to suit your particular congregation. It is no use just reading material straight from the outlines if people won't understand it!

Make a special note of any components which require advance preparation and organise accordingly. This will save you the stress and inconvenience of discovering at the last minute that someone has overlooked a piece of preparation crucial to the successful running of the service. Some resources and PowerPoint presentations are available (as free downloads) on the *All-Age Service Annual Vol 2* part of www.scriptureunion.org.uk/light. These may need adapting for your purposes.

If you are going to follow a recommendation to use a DVD clip, you will need to check its certification and obtain permission from the parents of young children for them to see the clip if necessary. You should also ensure that your church holds the relevant licence to show film clips; details of the Church Video Licence are available at www.ccli.co.uk. You may also want to use worship CDs/DVDs such as Hillsongs Kids CD/DVDs *Superhero* and *Superstrong God*.

You may find some of these services contain suggestions as to how to obtain images via the Internet for use in PowerPoint presentations or for other purposes. Please note that where websites do offer free images, they do so under certain conditions. In almost all cases, such images should be used for non-commercial purposes only. You have a responsibility to check for yourself the conditions involved, and the copyright status and owner of any image you should find by this means. Do not assume that any images on any site listed in this book can automatically be copied and shared with your congregation by any means without checking for further details and gaining permission where necessary. We have sought wherever possible to ensure that our suggestions fall within copyright law but Scripture Union does not accept responsibility for any copyright infringements by individuals using this book to prepare material for worship with their congregations.

Finally, in everything you do that is related to all-age worship, and even during the service, be open to the work of the Holy Spirit. Don't let these outlines and your planning around them prevent you from saying, doing or including something that you genuinely believe is from God. After all, he is the focus of our all-age worship!

THE
ALL-AGE
SERVICE
ANNUAL

Elisha 1

OCTOBER 2 Kings 4:8-37; Luke 17:11-19

Background

Christians have always believed in the healing power of God and have looked to the ministry of Jesus to give examples of this. Yet the healing touch of God was at work not only in the pages of the Old Testament too, but is also active in the world today. Time after time we see the amazing love of God at work in the lives of ordinary people, bringing wholeness and healing. Today's service is an opportunity for congregations to celebrate the way God heals, to think about our response, and to pray for people and situations in need of God's healing touch. This is the first of five outlines on the life and ministry of Elisha. You may prefer to begin the series with the next outline on the commissioning of Elisha.

The Old Testament prophets were occasionally involved in the healing of people (eg Moses: Nu 21:4–9; Elijah: 1 Kgs 17:17–24). This story of Elisha's encounter with the woman from Shunem is another example of God's power at work. The dramatic story of the healing of Naaman continues the theme in the fifth outline in this book.

Healing is more than what affects us physically. Those in the Christian community recognise the importance of healing in relationships (both personal and international), and the healing of memories and emotions. Our prayers will reflect these priorities and also include something of an environmental concern for the healing needed in the natural world around us as a result of poor stewardship of the earth.

 Link

Users of Scripture Union's *Light* curriculum resources focus in October 2008 on God as a protector and then as one who heals, using stories of Jesus, the healer, from Mark 7:31–37; Luke 13:10–17; 17:11–19. The story of Elisha's role in bringing a dead boy back to life is an Old Testament story to balance the New Testament focus.

Introduction

Ask the congregation to help you think about what healing means. Prepare the word 'HEALING' on seven large (A3 if possible) cards, one letter to each card. Explain that 'healing' means 'making things better or whole'. Explain that you are going to pass the letters around or place the cards around the room for people to write on each one a word or phrase, beginning with that letter, that is a way of making things better or whole. Ensure that there are marker pens available before this activity begins. Allow five minutes. Everyone does not have to write on every letter.

Give some examples of what might be written:

H Helping, Heating a cold room
E Encouraging, Embracing
A Asking God, Arranging a lift
L Living in peace with others, Looking after someone
I Interceding (praying), Ironing
N Never giving up hope, Not…….
G God's love, Gardening

The letters are to be collected up and brought to the front and displayed. Read some of the words and phrases out loud. Explain that healing comes in many forms, but Christians believe that God is the source of all things being made better. Explain the theme of this service, and, if there is to be an opportunity to receive prayer for healing later on, let people know at this stage so they can prepare their response.

Praise

There are many good hymns and songs for this service, including:
'What a friend we have in Jesus'
'Anointing, fall on me'
'Father, like rain from the skies'
'O Christ the healer, we have come'

Prayers of confession

If this service is taking place in the autumn, there will be plenty of colourful dead leaves around, so collect enough leaves for everyone in church to have one. Make sure these are good-looking leaves, clean, dry and not mouldy. If it is another time of year, a few days before the service, collect enough flowers for everyone in church, with enough time for these flowers to become dead ones. Note that dead flowers can be smelly and unpleasant so handle them with care.

Pass round a basket full of the leaves or dead flowers, asking people to take one. You may need several baskets. When everyone has a leaf/flower, ask them to think of words that describe their flower or leaf and to talk to their neighbour about this.

After a couple of minutes, ask people to tell you some of the words; you may get words like dry, crispy, brown, beautiful, amazing. One word you may or may not get with the leaves is 'dead'. Point this out and say that whilst all the other words may be true, actually this is a dead leaf or flower. Once it was alive but now its time has passed. It will decompose and become part of the earth.

Life moves on and sometimes we have to let go or put behind us things we have done that we wish we hadn't done or things that we wish had not happened. Ask people to think if there is something they need to let go of. It may be something they have done that displeases God, that we call sin. In order to let go of that, we need to ask God to forgive us. Remind people of the words of 1 John 1:8,9.

Invite people to bring their leaf or flower to the front and place it in a sack or bucket. Next to this, place a basket containing pieces of evergreen. Invite people to take a piece of evergreen as they leave their leaf, which represents a fresh start and receiving God's forgiveness, which never fades or dies. If there are lots of people, you will need several places for people to go to.

You could sum up this time of confession with the following prayer:

Living God,
Your life in us gives us fullness of life.

Help us to hold onto what is good and true, and follow what leads us into life.
Help us to let go of what holds us back.
Forgive us when we choose the wrong way;
Forgive us when we are attracted to the wrong things;
Forgive us when we hold onto what we ought to let go.
Forgive us and heal us.
Amen.

You could conclude with these words:

Thank you for Jesus,
Who speaks his gracious word to each of us, saying;
Your sins are forgiven; Go in peace.
Amen.

Reading the Bible

The following two passages from the Bible should be read aloud, by separate readers:

2 Kings 4:8–37
Luke 17:11–19

The story of the Shunemite woman in 2 Kings could be presented with parts read by a narrator, the woman, Elisha, Gehazi and the boy.

Bible talk

The teaching focuses around three phrases:
Asking God
Expecting God
Thanking God

You will need:
- A display board
- The words 'healing', 'God', 'asking', 'expecting', 'thanking' and 'for' on cards, large enough to be seen by everyone. The word 'for' needs to be smaller than all of the others.

Alternatively you can use the PowerPoint presentation prepared for this service found at **Elisha 1** www.scriptureunion.org.uk/light. If you use the PowerPoint version you will find

that the words 'asking', 'expecting' and 'thanking' keep moving around the screen, and at times will overlap. This is intentional and will enable you to point out that our experience of seeking healing ought to be a continual journey of asking, expecting and thanking.

Begin by placing the word 'healing' centrally on the display board and reminding people of the more general words that were used to describe healing earlier in the service – eg Helping, Encouraging, Asking God. Reiterate that healing comes in many ways, and through many people, including doctors and nurses, friends and neighbours, and people who pray for us. Stress the point that God is the source of healing and that Christians believe that God works through many people to make things better.

Introduce people to Elisha, saying that he was one of the people God used to make things better for many people. The name 'Elisha' meant 'God is salvation'. He lived his life in such a way that he showed that God was in control. When he healed people it was to demonstrate that God was powerful and cared for ordinary people, not to show how great a man he was.

Summarise the story of Elisha by using the four people who read the parts in the reading. You may want to introduce each character before the reading and could even give each of them a large name badge. What can the congregation tell you about what happened to each of these people in the story?

Go back to the display board where the word 'healing' is displayed centrally. Remind the congregation that God was the one who healed in both the story of Elisha and the story of the lepers. Place the word 'God' above the word 'healing'.

Suggest that there are three other words around both stories that are important. The first is **Asking**. Place that word on the board to the top left of the word 'God'. Add the word 'for' between the words 'God' and 'healing', so that the board displays '**Asking** God for healing'. (If you are using the PowerPoint version these things will happen as you click the mouse.) In each story, people needed to **ask** God to make things better. The woman whose son had died **asked** the only one she believed could help, Elisha, the 'holy man of God' as she had called him. In the gospel, the ten men with leprosy **asked** Jesus, calling out 'Jesus, Master, have pity on us'.

When we need God to make things better, either for us, or for someone else, the first thing we should do is **ask**. Point out the sentence 'Asking God for healing'. If you are using the PowerPoint version, you will see that the word 'Asking' begins to move around the central words when you click the mouse.

Expecting Place this word on the board, towards the top right (or click again for the

PowerPoint version). Point out the sentence 'Expecting God for healing'. In both stories there was an element of **expectation**. Elisha **expected** something to happen, even after his servant, Gehazi, had been unable to help the child. Elisha believed and expected God to make everything better for the woman and her son. The men who had leprosy also showed **expectation** by doing what Jesus had told them when they made their way to the priests.

We need to **expect** something to happen once we have asked God to make things better. We need to have faith and put our hopes into action. If you are using the PowerPoint version, notice how the words move around and sometimes overlap. Asking and expecting God are very often linked to one another.

Thanking Place this word on the board at the bottom, or click the mouse if using PowerPoint. Point out the sentence 'Thanking God for healing'. Remind everyone how the woman was **thanking** Elisha as she fell at his feet, bowing before him. Remind them too of the one man who came back to **thank** Jesus for being healed from leprosy. The other nine failed to do so.

We always need to remember to **thank** God. If you are using the PowerPoint version, notice with the congregation how the words sometimes overlap. This reminds us that seeking healing from God is often a journey through **asking, expecting and thanking,** where there are many blurred edges. Notice though, that God remains central.

The stories of Elisha and the ten lepers help us realise that God is the one who can heal, but that we have our part to play also. We should ask God, expect God, and thank God whenever we come seeking healing.

Prayers of thanksgiving

Thanksgiving is a natural response to the Bible teaching. The following prayer needs one main leader, and seven other readers of all ages with a line each. Print and highlight appropriately a copy of the prayer for each person so they can see where their highlighted line comes. The seven people could read from where they are sitting so long as everyone can hear; otherwise they should come to the front. Teach the congregation the bidding and response:

Leader: Loving God, we thank you for your healing
ALL: **We thank you for our wholeness**

Voice 1: When we don't know where to turn to and hope seems to be gone
Leader: Loving God, we thank you for your healing
ALL: **We thank you for our wholeness**

Voice 2: When we don't like our friends, and love seems to be gone
Leader: Loving God, we thank you for your healing
ALL: **We thank you for our wholeness**

Voice 3: When we don't feel well, and health seems to be gone

Leader: Loving God, we thank you for your healing
ALL: **We thank you for our wholeness**

Voice 4: When we don't see the way ahead, and direction seems to be gone
Leader: Loving God, we thank you for your healing
ALL: **We thank you for our wholeness**

Voice 5: When we don't feel alone any more, and doubt seems to be gone
Leader: Loving God, we thank you for your healing
ALL: **We thank you for our wholeness**

Voice 6: When we don't feel afraid any more, and fear seems to be gone
Leader: Loving God, we thank you for your healing
ALL: **We thank you for our wholeness**

Voice 7: When we don't feel unwell any more, and pain seems to be gone
Leader: Loving God, we thank you for your healing
ALL: **We thank you for our wholeness**

ALL: **AMEN**

Prayers of intercession

The prayer time should give an opportunity for people to receive prayer for healing. As all ages will be present, think carefully about the way this is done, and give an explanation with appropriate language. The way of receiving prayer given here is a simple, symbolic means of people receiving God's touch, which may be appropriate for people of every age, and is based on the biblical use of oil as a sign of God's healing touch.

Remind people of the three words **Asking**, **Expecting** and **Thanking**. Encourage everyone to think of something they need to ask for, something they are expecting God to do, and things they have to be thankful for.

Read James 5:14
Is any one of you sick? He should call the elders of the church to pray over him and anoint him with oil in the name of the Lord.

You will need a small bottle of olive oil. Explain that people in the Bible used oil because it represented God's healing touch. They would put some oil on the forehead of the sick person and ask God to make them better. Today we are going to pray in a similar way, but instead of our foreheads we are going to place oil in the shape of a cross on our palms to remind us of Jesus, who is the healer.

Ask everyone to place their hands on their laps, making a shape like a bowl. As they close their eyes, ask them to consider the question 'Where would you like to see God's healing?' Remind them gently that it may be something personal, or for another person, or for a situation where there is conflict or difficulty in the world.

After a moment, remind them of the Shunemite woman who went to Elisha so she could bring her prayer before God. Play some quiet music, during which time people can come forward to receive prayer, cupping their hands as though they are wanting to receive from God. The people who have been prepared beforehand to pray with others should each have a small bowl containing olive oil and should make the sign of a cross on the palms of the person coming to them. There is no need to ask the person what it is that they need prayer for, but perhaps the words "May God's healing touch come to you" could be said as the oil is placed on the hands.

Close this time with an appropriate prayer. Explain how and when support is available for anyone who would like to talk with someone about what they have prayed about.

Response

Our response is the prayer for healing which has just been described. However, during this time some of the following songs might be an additionally appropriate quiet response.

'Be still for the presence of the Lord'
'For the joys and for the sorrows (For this I have Jesus)'
'There is none like you'

God's blessing

Go in the wholeness and healing of God the Father.
Go in the strength and peace of God the Son.
Go in the anointing and power of God the Spirit.
May God bring healing to all you pray for,
And through your lips and your life, may he bring peace.
Amen.

Elisha 2

NOVEMBER 2 Kings 2:1–18; Matthew 4:18–21

Background

This is the second in the series on the Old Testament prophet, Elisha, although you may choose to use this outline first, since it introduces him. Elisha was active during the ninth century BC but little is known about his background apart from what we are told in 1 Kings 19:19–21. Elijah, the tough prophet who had taken on the might of kings and queens and false prophets and triumphed in the name of God, went to find Elisha and appointed him as a younger companion. Elisha probably came from somewhere in the Jordan valley and was from a fairly well-off family. His initial call happened in the ordinary business of getting on with life, just like the call of the disciples (that we will hear about in Matthew's Gospel account) as they went about their job as fishermen. But the confirmation and equipping of Elisha for his task was far more dramatic and memorable.

God calls us all to follow and serve him. For most people that call is not a single, highly memorable event but an ongoing, repeated call that has lasting effects. Again and again in our lives as followers of Jesus we are reminded of what it means to serve him, and to serve him in the present. A call is not necessarily something for the future.

Most people have experienced taking on a task that is just right for them. Children may have experienced being appointed to a position in a sports' team which feels as though it had been made for them. Young people looking to begin work or take up a university place will look to see what is required of them. They want the position or course that is just right. Anyone looking for a new job will know all about job specifications. And that is what we will be focusing on in this outline. By the end of the service it is hoped that everyone will be challenged to take on a role that God has called them to, confident that because he has called us, we will be equipped to do the job!

 **Link**

Users of Scripture Union's *Light* curriculum material in November 2008 have been looking at the call of and promise to Abraham from Genesis 12–17. This service outline expands on this by looking at another set of people who have responded to God's call – Elisha and the disciples of Jesus.

Introduction

Explain that if you are a boss and you want to employ someone to do a specific job, you begin by looking at what the job needs and then write what is called a job specification for the ideal person you want to appoint. This will include essential qualities – for instance, a swimming instructor must be able to swim – and preferred qualities – such as, you would prefer him or her to own a car because they do need to teach in several pools in the area but they *could* borrow one. Explain that you are going to play a game of 'Guess the job' by announcing essential and preferred qualities for several jobs. Call a few people to the front to guess what the job is. Encourage everyone else to stand up when you announce each quality if it applies to them. They sit down if the next ones do not apply to them, whether they are essential or preferred qualities. How many of them would fit the job? For example, everyone who considers themselves strong stands up for the first one, and remain standing if they like flowers and vegetables, continuing to do so if they own a spade and a lawnmower. Everyone standing would be suitable for the job of…a gardener!

Essential: Strong; likes flowers and vegetables
Preferred: Owns a spade; owns a lawnmower
Job: Gardener

Essential: Goes to bed late; good at carrying lots of things at once
Preferred: Likes people and food; owns a strong pair of shoes
Job: Waiter/waitress

Essential: Runs fast; team player
Preferred: Good goal scoring record; prepared to train hard
Job: Footballer

Essential: Loves God; able to help people develop their gifts
Preferred: Leads worship; communicates well with children
Job: Church leader (amend as appropriate!)

Explain that we are going to look at what is needed to fulfil a role in being called to serve God.

Prayers of thanksgiving

Any new employee needs to listen hard when they first start a job, to discover what it requires of them and how the organisation works. Listening is all part of taking on new responsibilities. How good are we as listeners? Invite everyone to listen to a recording of some music or to hear it played by the music group. It should be a song which is full of what God has done that should make us thankful to him. For example: 'For the beauty of the earth' with the music by John Rutter or 'From the highest of heights to the depths of the sea'. What do people hear that makes them want to be thankful to God? Share comments and then offer a prayer of thanks for all that God has done for us.

Praise

Give out the notices for the coming week(s) and then ask everyone to pause to reflect on what has been happening in this last week and invite comments. How have they have seen God at work this week, in their own lives or in those around them? Have they seen a difficult situation resolved or an answer to prayer? You may need to have a couple of suggestions ready to share. This naturally leads on to a time of praise that God is with us and active. For example, you could sing:

'God in my living'
'God is an awesome God'
'God is good, we sing and shout it'

Prayers of confession

As you have been reflecting on the week past, people may have been reminded of things that have been said or done or which they have failed to do or say, all of which may have displeased God. Ask everyone to be quiet and think of anything that they have done that they know is wrong. Then show them a large plastic bottle filled with dirty water. Say that this bottle stands for all that they have just thought of. Dramatically empty the bottle out into a bucket and make a point of it being taken away to be tipped down the drain. Alternatively, hold up a pile of rubbish in a clean container which is dramatically emptied into a dustbin. The bin is wheeled out of church.

Then explain that the empty bottle and/or clean container are waiting to be filled with clean water or stuff that is not rubbish. That is like what happens when we ask God to forgive us. He takes away the wrongdoing, although we may still have to take responsibility for the effects of that. He then allows us to begin with a clean bottle/container. Read out Psalm 103:10–12 as a prayer declaring that when we say sorry, God removes our sin from us.

Prayers of intercession

Thinking of people starting new jobs, it would be appropriate to pray for those in new situations. If possible, create a photograph collage or a PowerPoint presentation of the people for whom you are going to pray. You could interview them to find out how they have got on and what they would like people in the church to pray for. You could invite everyone mentioned to come to the front, where the leaders of the church pray that God will equip them for their new tasks and the new situations they find themselves in. Each person could be given a card on which is written a Bible verse for encouragement. The people might include the following:

- Children who have recently started school for the first time or moved to secondary school, as well as students who have just begun their new term.
- Anyone who has recently begun a new job, taken on new responsibilities or is looking for a job.
- Anyone in world affairs or national or local politics who has taken on a new job, which might include the President of the USA.

Reading the Bible

2 Kings 2:1–18
Matthew 4:18–21

(Several readers should have been prepared beforehand.)
Introduce this by announcing that you have a job specification for someone in church today. Essential qualities are that they need to be able to read, have a clear voice and be willing to practise reading. The preferred qualities are that they did not read in church last week (because you want to involve as many people as possible) and that they love the Bible (preferred because the more that people read the Bible, the more they will learn to love it so this is a quality someone can acquire!). It might be interesting to see how many people would have stood up if you had asked who could lay claim to these qualities!

Then call up the prepared readers for these two readings. The reading from 2 Kings could be read as a script with a narrator, Elisha, Elijah and the group of prophets. Alternatively, everyone could join in saying Elisha's words from verses 2b, 4b and 6b. Put these words on an acetate or on a PowerPoint slide. Elisha was determined to stick with Elijah! You could also fill in the details of Elijah's initial encounter with Elisha in 1 Kings 19, when it was clear that he was being set apart for some significant task, indicated by Elijah placing his coat on Elisha.

In introducing Matthew 4:18–21, make a suitable connection between Elisha's call and the call of the disciples.

Bible talk

You will need either a PowerPoint template for three job specifications (a full version is available on **Elisha 2** www.scriptureunion.org.uk/light) or three templates on acetate or on a large sheet of paper.

Over the course of the talk you (or a volunteer) are going to complete three templates – one for 'A prophet to succeed Elijah', one for 'A disciple to go with Jesus', and one for 'A follower of Jesus in 2008/9'. If time is short, you could omit the disciple part of this talk.

Retell the first part of the story, explaining who Elijah was and what dramatic and courageous things he had done in obedience to God. He was about to die and someone was needed to take over his role. Consider what the job involved. You could ask for suggestions. These should include telling people how God wanted them to live, being God's representative in the community, occasionally being involved in God's miracles – remind people that Elijah had brought a boy back to life (which Elisha also did, as we saw in the first service outline) and had seen God bring fire down from the sky to burn up a very wet sacrifice on an altar.
So what sort of a person was needed for that job? This is a rhetorical question, although if the congregation is likely to respond well, invite suggestions. Complete the template along these lines:

WANTED: A PROPHET TO SUCCEED ELIJAH
Essential qualities:
- Spent time with Elijah, learning from his example and talking with him
  (Notice in the reading how Elijah and Elisha knew each other. Elijah had already shown Elisha, and those farming with him, that he had been chosen for a special task.)
- Believed in miracles
  (Notice that when Elijah caused the river to divide, Elisha walked across with him. You could retell that part of the story, rolling up a coat and pretending to strike the ground.)
- Unshockable
  (When Elijah was carried up into heaven – and you may need to retell this dramatic part of the story too – Elisha was very sad, but then he got on with what had to be done.)
- Listened to God
  (Notice how important this is for anyone to speak out God's words and truth.)

Preferred qualities:
- Prepared to be different
  (Elisha wanted to be seen to be different from the other prophets and anyway, prophets had to be prepared to stand out from the crowd – that's what a prophet does. People do not always welcome a word from God. A prophet had to be brave.)
- Aware of his own weakness
  (Elisha wanted to have a share of Elijah's power from God because he knew he would need it. He could not do anything without God's Spirit.)
- Persevering
  (Elisha was very committed to being with Elijah – as the repeated words in the reading will have brought out.)

Ask rhetorically, would you give the job of a prophet to Elisha?

(Another way to do this is to put up the list of essential and preferred qualities and see if the congregation can think of any examples from the passage. If not, use the ones in brackets above.)

More briefly fill in the job specification for the disciples using Matthew 4:18-21.

WANTED: A DISCIPLE TO GO WITH JESUS
Essential qualities:
- Love Jesus
  (Notice that they may not have known Jesus very well but Andrew had already brought Peter to meet Jesus – that's what John tells us.)
- Prepared to take risks
  (Jesus gave the disciples a strange command. They did not know exactly what it would

mean – how could they? – but they took the risk and left their fishing nets.)
- Prepared to be part of a team
  (Jesus called four of them together, and there were others.)

Preferred qualities:
- Prepared to listen to stories and to what Jesus said
  (This story is followed by the words that Jesus went around teaching and healing.)
- Prepared to learn from Jesus
  (From this moment they had a lot to learn and understand.)

Complete the job specification for being a follower of Jesus in 2008/9 by showing an empty job specification template with just the headings WANTED: A FOLLOWER OF JESUS IN 2008/9, 'Essential qualities' and 'Preferred qualities'. What sort of qualities does Jesus require for anyone who is to follow him? For inspiration, look back at the qualities for Elisha and the disciples. Answers should include willing to take risks, loving Jesus, willing to learn, a team player, awareness of weakness, in fact, most if not all of what applied to the two templates above.

You could ask someone to share what it means to them to be a follower of Jesus. Interviewing them is probably going to be the most natural way of doing this. Help them in their preparation not to use jargon and to speak in a way that connects with people of all ages. They may highlight what it means to be different, or how inadequate they feel but emphasise how God has equipped them.

Response

This is a way of expressing commitment afresh. Produce a 'Jobs in the church' list which could be announced by a town crier sort of character or on an acetate or PowerPoint slide. Jobs should be as diverse and as all-embracing as possible. For example: welcome team, taking the offering, counting the money, tidying up after the service/the children's or youth group, musicians, PA/data projector operators, refreshment providers, befrienders, noticeboard monitors, Bible readers, cleaners, gardeners, prayer supporters. Most of these could be done by someone of any age and spiritual maturity. But what would happen if someone offered to do something you felt was inappropriate? Be prepared!

Choose the jobs you want to highlight and make available and explain what the job specification is – the essential and preferred qualities.

An example of a card for people to fill in if they wish to offer to do a job is at the bottom of this page.

You could fill in the 'position' space if there are specific needs. This would limit who offers to do what. People can be invited to step forward to take a card/application to complete and place in a suitable container at the end of the service. Alternatively, when the collection is taken, as another form of offering ourselves to God, people could place their card with the monetary gifts.

God's blessing

Conclude by singing a song of commitment, such as:
'Father, let me dedicate'
'I want to serve the purpose of God in my generation'
'Take my life'
'I will offer up my life'
'Abba Father'
'Father I place into your hands'

You could use this prayer, said by two people:

Jesus said to his disciples, 'Come follow me!'
May you go with Jesus into a new week.
Be assured that Jesus said to his disciples, 'I am with you always, even to the very end of the age!'
May you know Jesus close with you throughout this week.
Amen.

_____ would like to be considered for the position of

_____

Signed _____

Date _____

Nativity Service

DECEMBER Isaiah 7:13–14; Micah 5:2; Matthew 2:1–11

Background

The nativity story is central to the Christian faith. God became a human being in order to identify with our humanity and ultimately to die an undeserved death in order to take the punishment for our sin. It is such a central story and yet it is usually only told at one time of the year, and often it is told incompletely or tied up with tales of Santa and Christmas traditions. This outline seeks to provide a flexible structure that could be used in a variety of contexts, with the aim of telling the biblical account of the Christmas story to people of all ages. It could be used in a church service one Sunday in December, or specifically as an all-age carol service, or in a church building as a journey experience made available for local schools and members of the community to participate in over a period of hours or days or in a school context. The overall theme of this outline is that of surprises! People were surprised again and again but as events unfolded their surprise began to make sense. This is the challenge to everyone present – in one sense we should be surprised that God became a human being, but in another sense we would expect that of a God who loves his world so much that he found a way to rescue humanity.

Note: if this is being made available for schools to use, you will need to ensure that it is appropriate for children of the relevant year group and ties in with the requirements of the National Curriculum and RE guidelines. It is not appropriate to put words into children's mouths that they do not understand and do not believe, nor should we make assumptions about what children know. The reality is that most have a fairly confused version of the Christmas story and this is a marvellous opportunity to tell the story in as straightforward a way as possible. If the church building is also open to the wider community to experience the nativity journey, it has been known for children to bring their parents or carers along to church, after school, so that people in their family can also hear the story!

The basic structure of this service is four scenes or 'stations' which will provide the focus for telling the story in four parts:

• a room in a carpenter's workshop
• the hillside behind Bethlehem
• the place where animals lived (the stable)
• a home where there is evidence of a toddler (where the wise men came)

If space allows, participants walk from one 'station' to another as the story unfolds. But if this is not possible, the different scenes could alternate from different sides of the stage at the front of the building, to give the impression of a change of scene. Carols and Christmas songs could be interspersed during the storytelling experience if this is a carol service. The outline provides the same range of components as all the outlines in this book but you will have to choose what is most suitable for this more unusual occasion.

Everyone is given an envelope or small bag to take with them on their journey as they collect 'souvenirs'. These 'souvenirs' are:

- a small piece of splinter-free wood or a burnt matchstick
- grey cotton wool to look like sheep's wool
- a piece of straw
- a gold chocolate coin

Everyone also needs to make a choice from a range of beautiful objects – for example from different coloured pieces of tinsel, different coloured stones or feathers, or a flower. They will give their chosen object back to Jesus as a symbolic gesture of giving to him something they find precious or attractive. Allow your imagination to come up with ideas as you prepare this service. Think about the lighting, the scents, the atmosphere that you can create to make this memorable for everyone. You could also provide some simple props for children to join in the story – tea towels for shepherds, ears for donkeys, long tails for sheep, walking sticks as shepherds' crooks.

The place of surprises is the way the Christmas story in *The 10 Must Know Stories* (SU) 2008 has been told, entitled 'Surprise, surprise'. The 'Must Know Stories' are the ten Bible stories that have been voted as the ones that must be passed on to the next generation. They have been written for adults, for 8 to 11s and for 8s and under. It is suggested that part of the Christmas story 'Family politics' in the adult book, *The Must Know Stories* is read during the service. The extract is available on **Nativity_1** www.scriptureunion.org.uk/light. You might consider giving the children's books away since they are especially aimed at those who are on the fringe of church. They are reasonably priced and bulk orders are possible. For more details see page 29 or ring 0845 07 06 006.

 **Link**

Throughout December 2008, *Light* users have been exploring God coming to his people in the first two chapters of Luke's Gospel. The series concludes with a session on Matthew 2:1–23 on the Sunday after Christmas. This service naturally fits into this.

Introduction

Welcome everyone, checking that the envelopes/bags to collect souvenirs during the journey have been given out. Explain how the service or journey is going to be organised. If appropriate sing an opening carol/song. The new *Carol Praise* published by HarperCollins*Publishers* has a great mixture of carols – old, new and revised ones too – for all ages.

The story begins…
Move into the first scene/station which is a carpenter's room. Make sure there is a comfortable chair, ideally a rocking chair, with a trestle table and evidence of wood and safe tools. You might want to scatter wood shavings on the floor but have matchsticks or pieces of wood ready to give to each person. Welcome people to Joseph the carpenter's workshop. He lived over 2,000 years ago. Make it clear you are only pretending to be Joseph. If there is a small enough group, invite people to touch wooden objects and ask people about their favourite tree or wood. It has been a busy day and you want to have a rest. Settle yourself down into a comfy chair. Invite everyone to rest with you, imagining they can smell the wood, can feel the smoothness of polished wood and the splinters to be found in rough wood. Encourage them to close their eyes to rest, breathing in deeply as though they are about to fall asleep.

Allow silence to fall and then a voice is heard through the PA system, maybe accompanied by soft music or the sound of wind, or a trumpet, or whatever you think might introduce an angel! This will need to be prepared beforehand. The angel says:

'Joseph, Joseph, are you listening in your dream? You are upset because Mary, your fiancée, is having a baby and you are not the father. But she is not making it up when she says that God is the father. That is true! Go ahead and marry her. Then after the baby is born, give him the name Jesus. That name means, "He will save his people from their sins".'

The leader wakes up and rubs his eyes. Did everyone hear what was said? Joseph heard an angel speak to him in a dream. He was so surprised! He had been surprised still when he heard that Mary was going to have a baby. He was even more surprised when she said that God was the father. And even more surprised when the angel spoke to him! Talk about surprises that people have had and then make sure everyone has been given a piece of wood to remind them of the surprise that Joseph had in his workshop.

But Joseph needn't have been surprised because prophets long ago had predicted that a young woman would have a baby, in the town of Bethlehem. This baby would be known as 'Emmanuel' or 'God with us'. Just listen to what is written in the Bible, words which Joseph would have heard many times:

Reading the Bible

Isaiah 7:13–14; Micah 5:2

Explain that Isaiah and Micah were both prophets of God who, over 700 years before Jesus was born, proclaimed the following words to God's people. Notice that this baby was to come from Bethlehem, which was over 100 km from Nazareth where Joseph lived. You will not need to read the Matthew story until the last scene/station.

This could be followed by a song such as: 'Come, thou long-expected Jesus' or one that includes the word 'Emmanuel' – God with us.

Prayers of confession

The story continues…

Explain that Joseph did what the angel told him – he married Mary, but then they both had to travel to Bethlehem, where Joseph came from, because the Roman authorities had ordered everyone to go to the place where their family came from, to put their name on a register. This was so that they could pay more taxes. By the time Joseph and Mary got there, Mary's baby was almost ready to be born. But when the baby boy was born, the only place to lay him down was in a box of hay, used to feed the animals. It would appear that there was nowhere better for God-become-human to sleep.

You could read an extract from *The Must Know Stories*, the story 'Family politics' which is Robert Harrison's effective and unusual retelling of the story from Joseph's perspective. Joseph had brought Mary to Bethlehem hoping that his (fictional) Aunt Ruth, a steely matriarch, would take pity on them, as culturally she would have been expected to do. She did let the couple stay but the house was full and by the time Jesus was born, Mary was afraid to sleep in the communal sleeping quarters for fear that her baby would be crushed. So he was put to sleep in the animals' feeding trough. (This extract is on the SU website – **Nativity_ 1** www. scriptureunion.org.uk/light.)

Alternatively, you could read part of the Christmas story 'Surprise, surprise!' from *The 10 Must Know Stories* by Heather Butler. This has been written for 8 to 11s and is also on the SU website – **Nativity_ 2** www.scriptureunion. org.uk/light

Joseph may have been surprised at how everything was working out. So often we are surprised when things work out differently from how we expect. We may complain and say that it is not fair.

Pause to ask God to forgive us for the times when we grumble or feel let down. We may be suffering injustice. But as Joseph discovered, God was keeping him and his family safe. God knew what was going on and it was OK, even though Jesus' life was anything but easy. Ask God to forgive us for the times when we forget to trust that God knows what is best.

Praise

Create scene/station two which is a hillside with sheep and shepherds. Invite any children who are participating to take their place. Use green floor covering, plants, rocks as well, with the grey cotton wool to distribute as a souvenir.

The story continues…

Joseph, Mary and the baby settled down for the night to recover, but shepherds out on the hills behind Bethlehem were in for a big surprise. Tell their story from Luke 2:8–20. These shepherds had been surprised by the angels but they were not surprised by what they found. It was just as the angels had told them.

Choose a couple of songs which reflect the praise of God offered by the angels. These could be appropriate worship songs or carols which tell the story such as:
'While shepherds watched'
'See him lying on a bed of straw'.

Bible talk

Create scene/station three which is the 'stable' with animals, a 'baby' in a box of hay, straw and the standard nativity scene with child participants. The straw can be given away as another souvenir.

The story continues…
The shepherds were not surprised, although they were still in shock! They told Joseph and Mary all about the angels. Complete this part of the story.

Joseph and Mary called their son Jesus. Their family may have been surprised by this name but we aren't surprised because we know what the angel told them to call the baby.

There have been lots of surprises, and there are more to come. People have always been surprised by Jesus. He made friends with people that others did not like. He healed people and performed miracles which surprised and amazed people. He told stories that had a surprising ending. He was put to death by his enemies when his best friends thought that could not happen. And he came alive again three days later, which completely surprised everyone.

Jesus still surprises people. He is now in heaven but his Spirit is with us. The Holy Spirit helps us see God's power at work in people's lives in surprising ways. He helps people to know God. He comes to people when they are lonely or sad.

But like Joseph and the shepherds we need not be surprised. This Christmas are you expecting God to be with you in a special way? If not, you may be in for a big surprise! If appropriate, ask someone in advance to say what it means to them that God became a human being and in what ways they are hoping God will help them this Christmas. They will need to speak in jargon-free language.

Prayers of thanksgiving

There is usually plenty to thank God for at Christmas time. You might like to do this all together, or invite people to write or draw their own comment to God. If you are doing this all together, create some smiley faces on a board or acetate with space to write down the cause for thanksgiving. If you are doing this more personally, give everyone a smiley face and invite them to write down or draw on it their cause for thanks. They can then put it in their envelope or bring it to the front, either in this part of the service or at the end in the 'Response' section.

Prayers of intercession

At this time of year there are some who have been surprised by personal tragedies or national or international disasters. There may of course be pleasant surprises too, such as a baby arriving early or a visitor turning up unexpectedly. It would be appropriate to pray for these people/situations. If possible, create visual images so that it is clear that this is present-day reality. Invite a group of people to lead in prayer.

Response

Create scene/station four, which is a room with toys and clothes you might expect a toddler to have. You will also need a 'symbol' for something that is precious, as were the three gifts brought by the wise men, plus a gold coin to give as a souvenir to everyone. Keep the box of hay from the previous scene which will symbolise Jesus or, alternatively, have a lighted candle to represent him (but ensure that it is safely placed and away from children and flapping clothes).

The story continues…

Jesus grew up and became a toddler. One day some travellers from another country far away called by. This is what they had to say: Read Matthew 2:1–11. They were surprised that a king was not to be found in a palace in Jerusalem. But when they found Jesus, they were not surprised to see a young child and they recognised him as the king they had been looking for. Explain the meaning of the gifts: gold for a king, incense for worship and myrrh which was used in burial. If you have a small group, let everyone smell frankincense and myrrh, if possible showing them what they looked like. Give everyone a gold coin souvenir.

These wise men gave to Jesus something that was very precious, that they valued. This was their way of worshipping God, showing how much they valued him. We worship God by singing and praising him but also by living lives that please him. As a symbolic gesture, explain that everyone can pick one stone/feather etc from a basket, choosing the one that they like the best. They can then bring their stone either to put in the box of hay or else to put beside the lighted candle, the significance of which has been explained. (This will need to be done with great care, perhaps with someone standing by to ensure safety.) This represents Jesus. As people do this, they can say a statement such as the following: *Jesus, I want to give the best to you.*

(This response would not be appropriate in an educational setting. It would be more appropriate for them to say: *The wise men gave their best gifts to Jesus.*)

God's blessing

Everyone either returns to the scene/station which they like best or everyone stands with their hands held out to receive from God. When everyone is ready, use the following words:

Expect God the Son to give you joy.
Expect God the Father to show you his love.
Expect God the Spirit to make you strong.
And may God surprise you all!
Amen.

THE
**ALL-AGE
SERVICE**
ANNUAL

Christmas Day

DECEMBER Isaiah 9:6–7; Luke 2:8–20

Background

Christ was born into a disappointed world – hardly a theme we would normally dwell upon at Christmas, with all the tinsel, music and fun, carol services, parties and presents! But God's people had been waiting for the Messiah to come for centuries. How much longer did they have to put up with waiting? They now found themselves incorporated into the mighty Roman Empire. Where was the dream of being God's people, freely living in their own land? The religious authorities imposed their rules and regulations so those who were true worshippers, such as Zechariah, Elizabeth, Simeon or Anna, must have felt oppressed by such a regime. Where was God in all this? There were plenty of grounds for deep disappointment.

Disappointment might be one way many people describe their lives. Some children and young people might identify with that too. Life is not what we wish it would be. Actually many people are disappointed by their experience of Christmas – things go wrong, expectations are unrealistic, families together for an extended time in abnormal circumstances bring additional pressures, so disappointment is almost inevitable! The prospect of a new year may be depressing rather than hopeful. But the message of Christmas is that God came into this world to offer hope! He offers hope to our disappointed world now! This service outline explores this theme.

In an all-age Christmas Day service, the congregation may be more mixed than at any other time in the year – mixed in terms of ages, commitment to the church and commitment to God. There will be many unchurched or fringe people who come with their families or because this is one religious tradition that they honour. Who should be your target audience? Probably you want to cater for everyone in one way or another, by combining traditional elements of Christmas with fun and enjoyment, yet reminding everyone that God came to his people in the incarnation and continues to come to those who welcome him today! A short service may be what you are looking for, so select the components that best suit your purpose.

 **light Link**

Throughout December 2008, users of Scripture Union's *Light* curriculum material have been exploring God coming to his people, using the first two chapters of Luke's Gospel. This service continues the theme. The series will conclude with a session on Matthew 2:1–23 on the Sunday after Christmas.

Introduction

You will need to create a large object that is clearly visible, interesting in shape and which you fall over every now and again. It is wrapped up in paper or material with interesting things stuck on it. In fact it contains only one unlit candle (or your Advent ring) which will look very small when it is finally uncovered. (Disappointment might be one way to describe this unveiling! It promises so much but does not deliver!) You need to be able to remove a few layers or boxes over the course of the service before revealing the candle at the end! Give this object a name such as 'Giant green mountain' if it is large and mountain-shaped and covered in green cloth. (We will refer to this object by this name during the rest of the service outline.)

Most children will have opened at least some of their presents and may have brought them to church. Begin by finding out what presents people have had and share in their pleasure. But not everyone will be so pleased. Some people may have been expecting a gift they had asked for and no one has given it to them. Or it may be the wrong size or colour. Children may prefer the present given to a sibling or friend.

People may not own up to being disappointed but, if you can, interview someone who this Christmas, or on a previous one, ended up disappointed. Talk about how it felt and what they did about it. For example, for Christmas 2007 a lady bought her husband a beautiful olive wood chess set from Provence which is a part of France they love. She was thrilled to be giving him something so special that she knew he wanted! On Christmas Day her husband gave her a mystery, large, heavy box and inside was… a beautiful ceramic chess set! It was funny and went down in the annals of that family's history. But her disappointment was huge, both as someone who had given a gift and someone who had received one!

Explain that Christmas can sometimes be disappointing and that is what you are looking at in this service.

Praise

Sing a traditional carol which is well known by everyone. *Carol Praise* (HarperCollins*Publishers* 2006) is a brilliant collection of carols old and new, and some with an interesting twist. It might be worth introducing one new carol this service, but only one.

Arrange for someone to come rushing up to the front carrying a letter or holding their mobile. Either in the letter or on a text is the following message: Don't look inside 'Giant green mountain' until I tell you!

Reading the Bible

Isaiah 9:6–7
Luke 2:8–20

Before reading from Isaiah, explain that 700 years before Jesus was born, the prophet Isaiah gave this prophecy about the arrival of a special ruler from the family of David. (We know that this was Jesus.) This meant that God's people had to wait a long, long time – far longer than

waiting for Christmas to arrive this year. Ask rhetorically if people might have felt like giving up waiting or even have felt disappointed that God appeared not to have kept his promise. Had he forgotten them?

You could read the Luke passage here or as part of the Bible talk.

Bible talk

Arrange for another person to come rushing up to the front carrying a letter or holding their mobile. Either in the letter or on a text is the following message: Don't look inside 'Giant green mountain' until I tell you!

Fall over the large object and get cross with it. 'What on earth is this?' you ask exasperated. 'But I mustn't look inside it!' But you do remove a bit of wrapping, just a little, to build up the suspense.

Explain that you are going to hear about three people who were around at the first Christmas and they all knew what it was like to be disappointed. The first person is Joseph. If needs be, explain that an angel had told Joseph, a carpenter, that his fiancée, Mary, was telling the truth when she said that God was the father of her child who was going to be the special ruler promised by God through the prophet Isaiah. This was a bit of a shock for Joseph! He hadn't even married her yet! But then Joseph was ordered by the Romans to leave his home in Nazareth and travel over 100 km to Bethlehem. Here is what Joseph had to say about what happened:

(Arrange either for a man to read this out with suitable background noises or record it with the background noises.)
'My name is Joseph. I was hoping that we wouldn't have to stay long in Bethlehem so I could get back to my carpentry shop. (*Banging and sawing noises.*) You see, the Romans ordered everyone to go to the town where their family came from, to be put on a register. This was so that the Romans could make us pay more taxes. I had to go to Bethlehem. I closed up my carpentry shop, and my fiancée, Mary, and I travelled from our village in the north all the way down to Bethlehem. (*Introduce donkey clopping sounds.*) When we got there, I thought there would be somewhere to stay but, to my disappointment, there was no room. Mary was about to have the baby so I was really fed up that we couldn't find anywhere to sleep. You can't have a baby standing up! (Actually you can but I didn't want that to happen!) I began to panic. Eventually I found a family who said we could sleep where they keep their animals. It was warm and safe.

But it was all a bit disappointing!'
Arrange for yet another person to come rushing up to the front carrying a letter or holding their mobile. Either in the letter or on a text is the following message: Don't look inside 'Giant green mountain' until I tell you! You trip over it again and get cross again! Remove a bit more wrapping.

But here's another disappointed person:
(Arrange for a shepherd to come in, suitably clad, with background noises or record him speaking these words with the background noises.)
(*Create wind noises and sheep baaing.*) 'I am the youngest of a group of shepherds looking after a load of scruffy sheep on the cold hills behind Bethlehem. It was a very sharp night and I was tired. The others were whispering about the Romans, even though there wasn't a soldier in sight. But then, you never know who to trust these days. And suddenly the sky was sparkling and dazzling and there was loud singing and we were all on our feet about to run! (*Background angelic music!*) And out of all this noise came a voice, an angelic sort of voice. "Don't be afraid! A Saviour has been born for you! He is Christ the Lord. You will find him dressed in baby clothes and lying in a bed of hay!" More singing and more dancing and then we were off. Not to run away but to go down to Bethlehem to see what was going on. A Saviour wrapped in baby clothes, lying in a bed of hay!

'It was most strange. But I was a bit disappointed because this Saviour, the special ruler that the prophet Isaiah told us about 600 years ago, was only an ordinary skinny baby, wrapped up tightly so we could just see his face and, well it wasn't much at all. (*More baaing.*) But his parents were very peaceful and welcoming and somehow it felt very special. We told them about the angels and as we told them it all sounded pretty amazing. Then we went back to work. But what sort of a Saviour is that? How can a baby save you? I am puzzled, although I know something extraordinary is going on.'

And here is the last disappointed person:
(Arrange for an old man to read the following, dressed as Simeon with suitable background

noises, or make a recording of this with the background noises.)

'My name is Simeon and I have been living near the temple in Jerusalem for years and years and waiting and waiting for the Saviour, the special ruler that the prophet Isaiah told us about 600 years ago, to arrive. Now that we are ruled by the Romans it has become so hard to believe that he will ever come. I have been told that I will not die until I have seen this Messiah. But it has been disappointing. How much longer do I have to wait?

'But a few days ago, God's Spirit told me to go into the temple. Coming towards me I saw a mum and a dad clutching a new baby. (*A baby crying, which can be quite poignant since it emphasises Jesus' humanity.*) And as they came towards me, God's Spirit told me that this baby was the Messiah, the one promised from God, the one who would save us, the special ruler. I could hardly contain my excitement. The parents, who were called Mary and Joseph, handed the baby to me. I held him in my arms and thanked God for him. And I blessed the parents too. This was not what I had been expecting but here, at last, was God's answer! I was so thrilled and awed. At last, the Saviour had come. This baby!'

Three disappointed people. They had all been expecting something which was different from what actually happened. But none of them was disappointed by the end of the story. You see, at the time, lots of people were expecting God to help them. But they did not expect a baby to be the answer. And they would have to wait over 30 years before they began to see what all this meant.

God came in the form of a baby to a disappointed world. This baby was Jesus. He lived just like everyone else did at the time. He ate, slept, played with his friends, learnt to read and write, worshipped God, made furniture and doors, grew up and then… eventually he died a cruel death, accused by his enemies, humiliated… and then he came alive again. His birth, death and resurrection all happened to give us hope and joy. God's hope has come to his world in a new way and has never left it.

Conclude this section by singing a reflective carol. The words of 'It came upon the midnight clear' in The Jubilate Group version to be found in *Carol Praise* is particularly suitable. Here is verse 3, used with permission:

And those whose journey now is hard, whose hope is burning low,
Who tread the rocky path of life with painful steps and slow;
O listen to the news of love which makes the heavens ring!
O rest beside the weary road and hear the angels sing.

Prayers of confession

To introduce this you could read John 1:9–12 in a modern version. Comment that today many people do not welcome Jesus. He is not what they expect or want. They don't think they need him. They are not interested. They ignore him. Pray the following prayer:

Jesus Christ, you were born into this world and most people did not expect you or want you.

They were disappointed in you. They ignored you. But anyone who accepts you and believes in you becomes a child of God.

We are sorry that we have sometimes ignored you, Jesus, and done what is wrong. Please forgive us. Amen.

Prayers of thanksgiving

Use this prayer to help focus on why Jesus came to earth:

Generous God, who created such a wonderful world for us to enjoy, we thank you that you gave your Son Jesus to come into this world. *(Pause to reflect.)*

Loving God, who in Jesus was born into a family, we thank you for the joy of human love. *(Pause to reflect.)*

Patient God, who goes on loving us despite the fact that we sometimes ignore you, we thank you that you are always with us. *(Pause to reflect.)*

Powerful God, who in Jesus has brought hope and light into the world, we thank you that you give us hope for the future, to take away our disappointment. Amen.

Response

Arrange for someone to deliver this message: Open 'Giant green mountain' now!

Amidst mounting excitement, ask some children to help you unwrap your object. Express sadness and disappointment when you discover that the only thing inside is an unlit candle.

Point out any candles you may have in the church, including those on a communion table, an Advent candle or others that form part of a decoration. Why do we use candles practically, symbolically, decoratively or, if appropriate, as part of our worship? (You may use your Advent ring as the candle inside the 'Giant green mountain'.) One thing that Jesus said about himself was that he had come as the Light of the world (John 8:12). He came to show up darkness for what it was and to guide people. He was the Light that gave life, real life – and hope!

This candle may have been a disappointment; we expected something much bigger and more interesting. But it stands for Jesus and the hope that Jesus came to bring which is far, far bigger than we can ever imagine!

As a response, light the final Advent candle and/or light the candle that you found in the 'Giant green mountain'.

Prayers of intercession

Many people feel there is no hope in their world and they have nothing to look forward to. If possible ask a group of people spanning all ages (not necessarily a family) to prepare to pray:

• Pray for those in your community who are feeling lonely or without hope.
• Pray for a current situation in the world where life is especially hard.

• Pray that people in these places who know and love God will be looking out expectantly to see God coming to his people, in the same way that Simeon was waiting and expecting the promised ruler to come.
• Pray that your church in the coming year will proclaim to the world the message of the hope that Jesus brings.

God's blessing

Offer everyone a chocolate or piece of fruit. But before you give them out, explain that this 'gift' is a symbol of God's generosity. He gave us Jesus, who came at the first Christmas to give us hope. We receive this hope as God's blessing to us. Each person who gives someone else a piece of fruit or chocolate should be encouraged to say to them the words 'Jesus was born to give us hope.'

£3.99 each

£7.99

The Must Know Stories

The nation's most iconic stories from the world's best-selling book ever!

Daunted by reading the whole of the Bible? *The Must Know Stories* series retells the most important stories from the Bible in an intriguing, biblically accurate and exciting way that will capture your imagination for ever!
A great read whether you know these stories well or you're reading them for the first time. Well-written, entertaining and powerful stories for all ages. Buy for yourself, buy for a child or buy for a friend, and make sure we never lose these remarkable stories that have shaped our history!

Elisha 3 (New Year)

JANUARY 2 Kings 5:1–19; Matthew 3:1–12

Background

This is the third in the series on the Old Testament prophet, Elisha. The kingdom of Syria or Aram, just north of Israel, was an enemy of Israel whose power and might is much in evidence in 2 Kings 6 and 7 – see the fourth and fifth in this series. This is the background to the story of Naaman, the Syrian army commander, who in desperation crossed into enemy territory to ask Israel's God to heal him. At the time there must have been a truce between the two nations. God, meanwhile, had been equipping individuals to play their part in this story. They overcame their personal fear, and maybe disgust, to listen, respond and obey – with the end result that God was glorified.

God equips his people as an ongoing process, even before birth (Psalm 139:13–16) and continues daily in the lives of those who live for him (Heb 13:20,21). The congregation will encounter a Bible story in which God equips three people for specific purposes. He also prepares us to serve him. This is a very suitable theme for the start of the year.

 **Link**

Users of Scripture Union's *Light* curriculum material in January 2009 focus on God equipping his people to serve him, an appropriate theme for the start of the year. They will explore how Jesus was equipped for his ministry, as a 12-year-old (Luke 2:41–51), by his baptism (Matt 3:1–17), by his temptation (Matt 4:1–11) and the role of John the Baptist (Matt 11:1–19; 14:1–12). This Old Testament story highlights how God equips people to serve him.

Introduction

Explain that this service focuses on God who equips his people. He equips us to listen to him, to respond to him and to obey, so he will be glorified. This phrase is repeated throughout the outline.

Prepare a number of cards which contain words to describe situations that require specific preparations, such as 'Revising for a test', 'Going on holiday', 'Football match on Saturday', 'Cooking a meal', 'Christmas preparations'. Make three cards for each situation. If you want to illustrate these, the Internet should supply you with fun cartoons or images, or draw your own. On the back of each card write one step in the preparation: eg preparing for a football match, write 'Put on your kit', 'Do warm-up exercises', and 'Find a ball'. Invite people of all ages to come to the front, each to hold up one of the cards. In turn ask each half of the church to suggest a way to prepare for each situation. If what is suggested is written on the back of one of the three cards, that side scores a point. At the end of the activity, the side with the most points wins.

Indicate that in each situation the preparation is important to achieve the end result. God prepares us to serve him, which ultimately gives him glory. But, as the congregation will discover, we need to listen, to respond and to obey.

Prayers of thanksgiving

If this service takes place in January 2009, the time of thanksgiving will involve remembering God's goodness in 2008. But to reflect on God's activity in our lives in the past days or weeks is important at any time of year so adapt the material accordingly.

Prepare a large timeline to span the year from January to December. Alternatively, if you have a larger congregation and worship area, hang up A1 sheets of paper each with the heading of a month in the year. As a praise song is played, encourage church members to write a 'Thank you' to God, either on the timeline or the A1 sheets. Younger children could draw on smaller paper or make something from play dough.

If your church is too big for all participants to move around freely, use a roving mike to ask church members the things for which they are thankful and allocate volunteers to write their comments on the timeline or paper.

Praise

The sung worship should reflect the time of thanksgiving. In a few songs, thank God for what he has done, who he is and who we are together. Suggestions include:

'Blessed be your name'
'Give thanks with a grateful heart'
'How great thou art'
'Great big God'
'Be happy! (I'm gonna jump up and down)'
'Come on and celebrate'

Reading the Bible

2 Kings 5:1–19a
Matthew 3:1–12

Introduce the 2 Kings reading by explaining that this story focuses on three characters who were prepared by God to bring glory to him. Choose seven volunteers representing a variety of ages to read the parts of the different characters. Provide each with a copy of the Bible text in advance with their words highlighted. Practising this is recommended. The characters are: narrator; servant girl; King of Syria; King of Israel; Elisha; Elisha's servant; Naaman.

Matthew 3:1–12 should be read by the leader of the service. Introduce this reading by explaining that it focuses on someone who prepared the way for people to meet Jesus.

If you have children of pre-school age in the service and you have a copy of *The Big Bible Storybook* (SU), choose someone to look at both stories with them, during the reading of the Bible – pages 83 and 132. For more details see page 41.

Bible talk   . As a talk . not with actors

This part of the service includes a *Parkinson* style of chat show. In advance, choose three church members to play the parts of the servant girl, Elisha and Naaman. Allocate three chairs, one for each character, who appear one at a time. Players must be confident and good readers. You will also need four large pieces of card, or four OHT sheets, to display the words **listen**, **respond**, **obey** and **give glory to God** at the appropriate times in the talk.

The reading of God's Word speaks to us all in different ways. It is important to have an opportunity to share what God is saying. At the beginning, ask the congregation to tell you what they have learnt from hearing the Old Testament story. Be sure to ask children as well as adults. Explain that the story provides a good example of people who did three things: they **listened** to God and others, they **responded** to the situation around them and they took action (were **obedient**), all resulting in **God being glorified**. At this point display the words as stated above. You are going to meet these characters now.

(The servant girl (SG) enters.)
Leader (L): Hello and welcome to _____ church. We have just heard your story. You played a remarkable part in something that changed a man's life. But I'm sure that it was not easy for you. Can you tell us all about it?
SG: It's a pleasure to share my story. As a young girl from Israel, I was terrified when we heard that Syrian troops had invaded my country. Then they came to our village and I was taken away from my family and friends. I was really, really terrified. I was so young. But God was preparing me for something.
L: Tell us what happened.
SG: In Syria, I was taken to the home of Naaman, who was the commander of the Syrian army. I was to be the maid who looked after his wife. I was very shy and scared. But in Naaman's home there was another scary situation. Naaman had a dreadful skin disease which meant that he was considered unclean. His skin was all raw. How could he be an effective commander of an army looking like that and perhaps being infectious? I plucked up courage and told my mistress that if Naaman went to see the prophet Elisha in my country, God might heal him.
L: But this man had been responsible for taking you away from your family. Didn't you want him dead?
SG: No. God was speaking to me, and I had to listen and respond to what he was saying. God needed me to be obedient so he could use me.
L: This story has a great ending! So thanks for joining us. We now welcome the commander of the Syrian army, Naaman.

(Naaman (N) enters.)
L: Sir, I know that in this remarkable tale there may be some things that embarrass you. But could you tell me about it?
N: *(Looking embarrassed.)* Well at first I was too proud to listen and do what the prophet said. I have to confess, I wanted it all my way. I

wanted to get well again (having a skin disease like that was so dreadful and embarrassing!) but I wanted it to be done quickly, easily, like magic. But the prophet Elisha reminded me that God was preparing me for this amazing healing and that I had to listen to God's instructions and take action. That meant bathing in the most disgusting of rivers, the River Jordan, taking my clothes off like a little baby and getting wet all over.

L: But the Bible tells us that because you did listen and obey, you were healed.

N: Absolutely. Elisha truly is a man of God. I now know that his God, the God of Israel, is the true God. From now on, my family and I will worship only him. He healed me and saved me.

L: Is there anything you would like to say to your wife's servant girl?

N: I want to thank her for helping me and telling me about God's prophet, Elisha.

L: Thank you, Commander. Now time to meet our final guest, the prophet himself, Elisha!

(Elisha (E) enters.)

L: Elisha. You are a mighty man of God. Why did you ask Naaman to take a wash in the River Jordan?

E: Naaman wanted to do some heroic stuff so he could take some of the glory for his healing. But since it was God who would heal him, it is only just that God should be recognised and be given the glory. Naaman needed to be humbled.

L: You are a prophet, so a lot of your time is spent listening to God. What do you make of what happened?

E: I am very impressed with the maid here, who risked a lot for her master. I am also impressed that this Syrian commander was humble enough to listen to a servant girl and then follow my instructions. My job is to enable

people to get to know God better. Through Naaman, others may now worship him. God was preparing us all. Giving glory to God is what it's all about for me!

L: Thank you to all my guests. I'm sure you will join with me in thanking them and giving glory to the God who prepares his people.

(Round of applause.)

Display the four phrases and reflect on each one in the light of the story.

Listen: All three characters listened to God and to what he wanted for this situation. What is God saying to us as individuals and as a church?

Make time to listen to him this week.

Respond: A response was made to each situation. The servant girl responded to her master's need, Naaman responded to Elisha's instructions, Elisha responded to what God wanted to do. When God speaks, we must respond. What situations should we respond to in our lives, in church, in school or for the needs of the world? Are there changes we need to make? Are there things that need to be said or done?

Make time to respond to God this week.

Obey: The characters were obedient and did the right thing. God wants us to be obedient to him. What is he asking us to do as individuals or as a church in order to make a difference in the world?

Can you do something to make a difference this week?

Give glory to God: The result of obedience was that at least one man and his family who were foreigners (not from Israel) worshipped God.

Pray that your words and deeds will enable others to glorify God too.

Prayers of confession

John the Baptist encouraged people in Judea to turn away from their sins, as he prepared them to meet Jesus. He baptised people in the same dirty River Jordan. This confession time will enable the congregation to say sorry before preparing to listen to God in the subsequent response time.

Lead the following prayers and actions, allowing people to make their response out loud and together: **I am sorry Lord.**

Think back over the week, month or year gone by and bring your prayers to God.
(Cup hand over ear.) For the times when I didn't listen – to my teacher, my parent, carer, boss, work colleague, or partner. For the times I thought I knew best:
I am sorry Lord.
(Cup hand over ear.) For the times when I didn't listen to you; when I knew I was doing wrong but chose to ignore you. For the times I thought I knew best:
I am sorry Lord.

(Point to yourself.) For the times when I thought about myself before others or when someone needed help and I could have gone out of my way to make a situation better. For the times I thought I knew best:
I am sorry Lord.
(Open hands as if reading a Bible.) For the times when I didn't obey your commands or when I didn't love in the way you love, when I didn't forgive in the way you forgive and when I didn't praise you in the way you deserve. For the times I thought I knew best:
I am sorry Lord.
For the times when my words *(point to mouth)* and my actions *(hold hands out wide)* did not bring glory to you. For times when I let you down and the times I was ashamed to be your child. For the times I thought I knew best:
I am sorry Lord.
Lord, as we come before you now, saying sorry with our whole heart, please forgive us and cleanse us. Renew our minds with your Holy Spirit and help us to live our life for you this week. Amen.

Response

This activity is a response to the confession. You will need to give each person a small piece of blank paper, a gingerbread man shape cut out of paper, a foot shape, an envelope and a pen. (Note: 'Footnotes' can be bought in packs of 100 from some gift shops.) Before the service, place these items on pews or in the backs of chairs, or hand out as people come in.
1. Listen to God – play some quiet music, light three large candles (safely placed) to allow a sense of stillness. In the quiet, encourage people to be still, asking God to prepare them to hear from him. For the kinaesthetic learners or young children, playing with play dough will enhance the listening process, but don't let this become a distraction.
2. Respond to your situation – ask each person to think of one important place for them where they can serve God. Is it at home, school, work or somewhere else? On the blank piece of paper, draw the outline of this place. Then ask everyone to think of someone they can pray for, help, or give time to. Write the name of this person or draw them on the person shape.

3. Obey – ask each person to think what God might be asking them to do. On the foot shape, each person writes or draws something they can do to serve God in the place, or for the person. Put all three pieces of paper in the envelope. You might play some background music as this is done. The lyrics of the songs 'What do you want me to do?' by The Waterboys or 'Yahweh' by U2 are excellent as an act of commitment to God.
4. Lead a prayer to ask God that everyone will experience God's Spirit preparing them this year and that through obedience and service, **God will be glorified.**

The following songs could be used to conclude this section:

'I'm giving you my heart (I surrender)' Marc James (Vineyard songs 2000)
'Lord I give you my heart' Darlene Zschech (Hillsong)
'It's excellent to be obedient' Sammy Horner (Daybreak music 1992)

Prayers of intercession

The servant girl was taken away from her home to a foreign place. God had prepared her to serve him in this new situation. It is important to remember those whom God has called and equipped to serve him in other countries. If you have link missionaries connected to your church, prepare a PowerPoint presentation showing a picture and a couple of prayer points for each one. Make sure there are enough for children to engage with. Between each picture, write the words 'Lord, prepare the hearts and minds of your servants by your Holy Spirit, that they might listen to you, respond to their situation and obey, for your glory.' Encourage everyone to read these out when they appear.

Alternatively, prepare a display board or stations around the worship area with similar information. Allow church members to look at the stations and pray at their own pace for five or six minutes. Again write the words of the prayer onto card, or use an OHT/PowerPoint slide.

If you have no link missionaries, find out about the work done by an agency such as Christian Aid, Toybox or Tearfund. Each will send you an information pack on request. Use this to inform your display or presentation. Use the words of the prayer above.

God's blessing

The act of blessing is an encouragement to everyone to go into the week prepared to listen, respond and obey. Display the words of this prayer on a screen or in your order of service.

Each person turns to the left and puts their hands on the shoulder (or if they are very small, the back) of the person in front of them. All pray together, everyone repeating each phrase after the leader:

May God prepare you this week to listen to him (pause), to respond to the needs of the world (pause), to obey him through your words and deeds. (Pause.)
May God bless you and those you meet this week. Amen.

Turn around 180 degrees and repeat, placing your hands on the shoulders of the person in front of you and praying the blessing prayer. End the prayer with a big shout of AMEN!!!

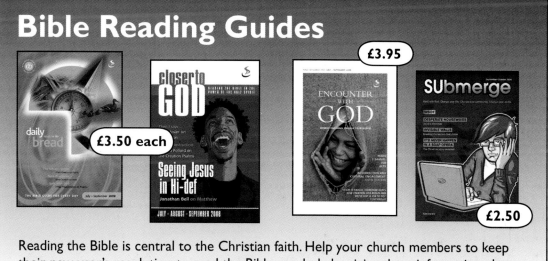

Elisha 4

FEBRUARY 2 Kings 6:8–23; 2 Corinthians 11:16–33; 12:9,10

Background

The dramatic Old Testament reading from 2 Kings can sound strange to modern readers. It takes place at a difficult time for the northern kingdom of Israel, following the split from the southern kingdom about a hundred years earlier. In the intervening years there has been great material prosperity, but much social injustice and spiritual weakness. Instead of worshipping the Lord and living in obedience to him they have started to worship a range of other gods. There have also been constant border skirmishes, so that despite the prosperity there has never been a time of complete peace. At the time of this incident Israel is at war with Aram (or Syria), a kingdom in the area currently occupied by Syria.

The fact that God knows what is going on and reveals this to his prophet Elisha should not surprise us. The role of a prophet is to hear from God and speak on his behalf. God still loves and cares for his people despite their sin and, in order to protect them, shows Elisha what is going on. Even when it doesn't look as though God is actively in control of events, he is caring for him.

The New Testament reading shows how God cares for Paul in a range of circumstances. Paul recounts these incidents to make it clear that he is in no way inferior to any of the other apostles or leaders. In doing so, he vividly describes what he has been through and how God faithfully looked after him on his travels.

Just because God looked after Elisha and Paul in those situations, we cannot assume he will make it possible for us to avoid tough situations we may face. But God's character has not changed so we can expect him to show his love for us by watching over us. This doesn't make us immune from the pain and suffering of this life. What is more, God's plans are not always the same as ours. There will be some in the congregation who have lost family or friends in tragic circumstances, who face chronic illness, family breakdown or unemployment. They may struggle with the idea that God always protects. So while we can have every confidence that God always has our best interests at heart, we have no right to expect that everything will turn out just as we want – Paul was beaten and stoned and eventually killed, but God looked after him. God was in control and was working to a bigger plan. Life is complex; as Tertullian, the second century Christian writer, said, 'The blood of the martyrs is the seed of the church.' Today the church in China is growing rapidly, but at great personal cost.

 **Link**

During February 2009, users of Scripture Union's *Light* curriculum material have been looking at the faithfulness of God through the story of Abraham (Gen 18–27). This outline on Elisha makes a link with this theme by showing that it is God's faithfulness that causes him to protect his people at the time of Elisha. This is the fourth in the series on the life and ministry of Elisha.

Introduction

Collect pictures of objects or people that offer protection, such as a castle, a rock, a cave, a syringe or bottle of medicine, some shin guards or cricket pads, a policeman or a soldier, a guard dog, a wall or fence, a sea wall or an insurance policy. If your church has the facility, display these via PowerPoint or on an OHT. A download of these images is available from **Elisha 4_1** www.scriptureunion.org.uk/light. If

that is not possible, either display the pictures big enough to be seen, or talk through the ideas without the pictures. Ask the congregation to say how each one acts as protection for us. Involve as many people as possible and from different age groups. Be prepared to comment on how these things provide protection and draw parallels with the way in which God protects his people.

Prayers of confession

As much of the rest of the suggested service is active and participative it would be good for this time of confession to be quiet and reflective. This is why it is placed near the start of the service, to avoid an abrupt change of mood, but it could be placed at other points. Alternatives might be to start with praise and thanksgiving, with the confession after the talk.

Choose music

Play a song such as 'Wonderful Grace' or 'God of Grace, I turn my face' and invite the congregation to think of times during the week when they have failed to trust God, have done things in their own strength, or have failed to go God's way

because they have believed their own way to be better.

At the end, pray using your own words, words of absolution from your tradition, the words of 2 Chron 7:14 or the following prayer:

Father God, we find it so hard to trust you with all of our lives and with everything that we do. So often we have behaved as if we knew better than you or were more powerful than you. We have not spoken up for you because we were afraid. We have gone with the crowd because it seemed easier. We are sorry. Please forgive us through your Son, our Saviour Jesus Christ. Amen.

Praise

Songs such as the following could be used either in blocks or interspersed between other items depending on your own preference. But it is important to find time to celebrate the goodness and the power of God:

'A mighty fortress is our God' (Some may not know this and the language and concepts are difficult for younger children, but it is a great hymn and well worth considering, if for no other reason than that it reflects the history of the Church and shows how others have experienced God's protection. It could even be introduced with some comments about Martin Luther and the way that God looked after him.)

Choruses

'Be still my soul'
'In the name of Jesus'
'Faithful One'
'When I walk through the valley' (Matt Redman)
'There is power in the name of Jesus'
'Living under the shadow of his wing'
'Our God is a great big God'
'The wise man built his house upon the rock'

- Jehovah Jireh
- Jesus stand among us

Prayers of thanksgiving

After Intercession

Use this responsive prayer based on phrases from Psalm 18. If your church is comfortable with it, finish with applause to show how much you appreciate what God has done. The prayer is available as a download from **Elisha 4_2** www.scriptureunion.org.uk/light

I love you, LORD God,
You make me strong.
You are the rock where I hide,
You are my strong castle,
You are the place where I am safe,
You are my shield, and my place of shelter;
I praise you, LORD!
I prayed, and you rescued me;
You are always faithful
to those who stick with you.

You, the LORD God, keep my light burning
and help me to see in the dark.
Everything you do is perfect, LORD,
and everything you say is right.
You always look after those who turn to you for help.
You alone are God!
You help me to run fast
just like a speeding deer,
and you help me stand
on the slippery mountain paths.
You are the living LORD,
I will praise you.
You are a mighty rock,
Thank you for keeping me safe.

Reading the Bible

Before reading the passages point out that after the readings you will be asking who God had protected, when he did it and where he did it. This will encourage people to listen carefully.

2 Kings 6:8–23
2 Corinthians 11:16–33; 12:9,10

Alternatively, there is a very powerful retelling of this story *'An invisible army'* in *The Strong Tower* (SU) by Robert Harrison which you could read instead of the 2 Kings reading. For more details see page 41 or visit www.scriptureunion.org.uk.

Bible talk

Depending on the nature of the congregation you may need to fill in some background to either or both readings to help people engage with the story. Then explain that in order to see how God protected his servants we are going to look at **who**, **when** and **where**. Write these three words on separate sheets or in columns on paper or slides, so you can write up responses on an OHT, flip chart or data projector.

Point out that you are going to look at both Bible readings together. Ask **who** God protects in these stories. There are some obvious answers – Elisha and God's servant, Paul. Others are less obvious – the nation of Israel, Paul's friends. (You may have to make the point that it doesn't look as though God protected Paul – but to come through all the things he lists was more than we would expect of anyone. If it helps, refer to his being let down the wall from Damascus (Acts 9:25); or being left for dead (Acts 14:19); or the way in which his nephew ensures that he is saved from the plot to kill him (Acts 23:12–22).) When you have a number of people identified, make the point that God protects all sorts of people.

Then ask, **where?** Again, some answers are obvious – Samaria, Dothan, Damascus. Others will be less obvious but some people may be able to name them such as rivers, roads and towns that Paul travels near. When you have a number of different locations, make the point that God can protect us in all sorts of places and situations.

Finally ask **when?** This is not a question about dates, although it might help to know that Elisha and Paul are separated by about 1,000 years. It is more about the sort of situations in which God is active – war, opposition, bullying, unfair treatment and so on. Comment that God can deal with a range of different situations. Point out that God acts in various ways. He tells Elisha what is going on in the enemy camp, surrounds him with angels and makes his enemies blind for a time. He saves Paul when his friends lower him over the wall in a basket. You will be able to find other examples from the readings.

Conclude by explaining that just as God cared for and protected his people then, so he cares for us and can protect us in the situations that we face. Refer to Paul's statement that when he felt weakest, he was actually strongest because the only thing left was God. It is when we rely on God, not on ourselves, that we will find his strength.

You could finish by learning 2 Corinthians 12:9 together. One way to do this is to put the whole verse on the screen and read it together a number of times, gradually taking away words until the congregation can recite the whole verse without any words on view.

(As part of the talk you might want to offer some help or even offer a few other verses for people to look at which illustrate some of the incidents that Paul mentions – these could be displayed on the screen or handed out on sheets of paper at the beginning. The following might be useful: Acts 14:19–20; 16:22–24; 19:23–31; 23:12–22; 27:27–44.)

Prayers of intercession

Make a large rock shape out of card, paint it grey and put it in a place that is visible to most of the congregation. Before you start this section distribute small slips of paper – perhaps with larger ones for young children. Make sure there is an adequate supply of pencils, pens and felt tips. You will also need Blu-tack. A large congregation may need two or more 'rocks'.

Give the congregation a few minutes to think about situations in which they, or others they know, might need God's protection or need God to look after them. Family groups, especially where there are young children, could work on this together. Young children present who are not part of a family unit within the church will need the support of other adults to help them. Ask them to write or draw the situations on the pieces of paper.

Read Psalm 18:1–3 and invite people to stick their papers on the 'rock'; making it clear that they can opt out if they prefer, but encourage participation. Select some of the comments/ drawings to read out or to describe.

This may involve some sensitive discussion with children about the content of their pictures. 'What is this?' is not a good opening! 'I like that; tell me about it,' is more likely to get them talking. Close with a prayer which offers all the individual prayers to God.

[handwritten: Image of wailing wall]

[handwritten: Music]

*[handwritten: Followed by Thanksgiving *]*

Response

This could follow straight on from the prayer activity, either standing on its own, or as an alternative way of bringing the time of prayer to a close.

'St Patrick's Breastplate' is an old, traditional prayer which exists in several forms. Use the version which is reproduced here. This could either be read by selected readers or put on the screen or service sheet for all to say together as follows:

All:
I arise today
Through God's strength to pilot me,
God's might to uphold me,
God's wisdom to guide me,
God's eye to look before me,
God's ear to hear me,
God's word to speak for me,
God's hand to guard me,
God's way to lie before me,
God's shield to protect me,
God's host to save me

Reader:
From snares of devils,
From temptations of vices,
Against inclinations of nature,
From everyone who shall wish me ill,
Far away and close at hand,
Alone and in a crowd.

All:
Christ with me, Christ before me, Christ behind me,
Christ in me, Christ beneath me, Christ above me,
Christ on my right, Christ on my left,
Christ when I lie down, Christ when I sit down, Christ when I arise,
Christ in the heart of every man who thinks of me,
Christ in the mouth of everyone who speaks of me,
Christ in every eye that sees me,
Christ in every ear that hears me.

Salvation is of the Lord,
Salvation is of the Lord,
Salvation is of Christ.
May your salvation, O Lord, ever be with us.

God's blessing

There seems no better way to conclude than by using the blessing from Numbers 6:24-26. This could either be given by the leader or it could be on the screen or service sheet with the congregation being invited to bless one another:

The LORD bless you
and keep you;
the LORD make his face shine on you
and be gracious to you;
the LORD turn his face towards you
and give you peace.

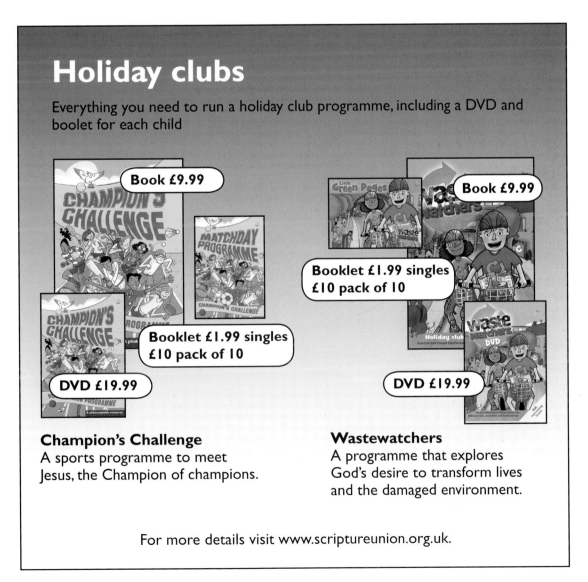

Holiday clubs

Everything you need to run a holiday club programme, including a DVD and boolet for each child

Book £9.99

Booklet £1.99 singles
£10 pack of 10

DVD £19.99

Book £9.99

Booklet £1.99 singles
£10 pack of 10

DVD £19.99

Champion's Challenge
A sports programme to meet Jesus, the Champion of champions.

Wastewatchers
A programme that explores God's desire to transform lives and the damaged environment.

For more details visit www.scriptureunion.org.uk.

Mothers' Day

MARCH Psalm 34:1–10; Luke 13:10–17

Background

Mothering Sunday was originally the day in the year for people to visit their parish cathedral – or Mother Church. Later, it came to refer to the Sunday three weeks before Easter when young women in domestic service would return home (with a simnel cake) to visit their mother before the busyness of Easter. These days it is a day for showing our appreciation to mums, through the giving of cards and gifts. Families have different traditions surrounding Mothers' Day – some children serve their mum breakfast in bed and older children may take her out for a meal. Whilst few would doubt that Mothers' Day is a huge commercial spectacle, it can actually be quite painful for many people. Be aware of this in your planning. You may also have a number of unchurched visitors joining you, so take care to use jargon-free language and explain things which those steeped in Christian culture take for granted. You may want to have literature available for such visitors to explain what Christians believe.

The aim of this service is to celebrate the goodness of God (particularly in the love shown to us by mothers and those who care for us), exploring the words of the psalmist and the actions of Jesus. There will also be the opportunity for your community to share their own stories of God's goodness.

But God's goodness is not just in his kindness. It is also that he is morally good. He is opposed to what is evil. He does the right thing. That will be touched on in the talk when there is the contrast between Jesus' goodness and the evil spirit in the woman. In addition, Jesus did the right thing even though the religious authorities objected strongly. Goodness in terms of doing what is right is not necessarily the same as a child being urged to be good in order to please parents or carers or teachers, which can have a 'meek and mild' connotation. We want to present God's goodness as anything but passive. Of course, parents have a responsibility to show their children how they should live rightly, both by what they say and by the example they set. In this respect, mothers and fathers certainly demonstrate God's goodness in doing what is right.

 Link

Users of Scripture Union's *Light* curriculum material in March 2009 explore Jesus' role in teaching and training his disciples and audience, looking at the parables in Matthew 13 and Jesus' encounter with children who were brought to him in Mark 10:13–16. The role of parents in nurturing their child(ren) and demonstrating God's goodness to them is a natural link with this service outline.
Note: Mothering Sunday or Mothers' Day occurs at various times in the calendar around the world. In the UK it takes place during Lent which is why this outline is linked to the March *Light* material. Use this material as appropriate for your country.

Introduction

Welcome everyone, especially any who are new or just visiting. Acknowledge that some people in the congregation may be suffering from MDOS – Mothers' Day Overload Syndrome! Reassure everyone that you intend to limit the fluffy side of Mothers' Day imposed upon us by retailers. At the heart of Mothers' Day is a celebration of something good. The fact that there are people in the world who care for us and do the right thing is definitely worth celebrating, but we also need to remember and celebrate the source of this goodness. God is good – he doesn't have good moods and bad moods, he doesn't 'do' good things from time to time. By his very nature, he is good! We know then, that when we are touched by goodness, the good Lord is behind it.

Explain that you are going to play a game to test people's knowledge of the creators of, or the people behind, some great inventions and works of art. Ask people to raise a hand if they think they know the answer to your questions. Add to or improve upon the list of artists /inventors below.

Q. Who was the person/people behind each of the following?
Penicillin – Alexander Fleming
Frozen food – Clarence Birdseye
The play, *Romeo and Juliet* – William Shakespeare
The World Wide Web – Tim Berners-Lee
The Lion, The Witch and The Wardrobe – C.S. Lewis

The painting, *Sunflowers* – Vincent Van Gogh
The *Harry Potter* books – J K Rowling
iPod digital music player – Apple Computers Inc
The ballpoint pen – Laszlo Biro
The *Artemis Fowl* books – Eoin Colfer
The painting, *Guernica* – Pablo Picasso
Email – Ray Tomlinson
The album, *Hot Fuss* – The Killers
The painting, *Girl with a Pearl Earring* – Jan Vermeer
Lego – Ole Kirk Christiansen
The album, *X* – Kylie Minogue
DNA fingerprinting – Alec Jeffreys
The painting, *The Haywain* – John Constable
The play, *The Importance of Being Earnest* – Oscar Wilde
The creator of the *Star Wars* films – George Lucas
Thomas the Tank Engine – Rev W Awdry
Bob the builder – Keith Chapman
You?

In much the same way that there is always an artist behind every work of art, or a musician behind an album, or an inventor or scientist behind great discoveries, there is a someone behind you! – mothers, fathers, carers, grandparents or any of those people who care for us and make us feel good! Behind all of the great people in our lives, however, there is the ultimate source of goodness – God! God is good, both in the way he is kind, and also in the way he does the right and good thing.

Praise

'Let everything that has breath, praise the Lord' – Matt Redman
'Wonderful maker' – Matt Redman (great lyrics for this service)
'Thank you for saving me' – Delirious?/Martin Smith
'Let your glory fall' – Matt Redman
'Amazing grace' – John Newton
'God is good, we sing and shout it' – Graham Kendrick

Reading the Bible

Psalm 34:1–10
Luke 13:10–17

These Bible readings were written by the psalmist, probably King David, and by Luke, the doctor who travelled with the apostle Paul. Both of them had experienced God's goodness and his help to do the right thing. You will hear how they communicated this in what they wrote.

Ask an older member to read the psalm and a younger person to read the story from Luke. You could find an appropriate image to accompany each of these readings to display on an OHT or PowerPoint – one of a royal or military figure to depict King David (Psalm 34), and one of a woman bent over or even in a wheelchair for a more contemporary take on the story (Luke 13).

Prayers of thanksgiving

You will need a flip chart, an OHT or PowerPoint facilities. Ask people to call out good things for which they are grateful. Write these down on the flip chart or OHT. Give some suggestions to get people started, such as parties or family.

You could create a two minute PowerPoint presentation of church-family life which includes photographs of people in the church and some recent events in the church. This would serve as a great visual reminder of how we experience God's goodness through belonging to one another. It may be of interest to visitors too but if you think it would exclude them, miss it out!

Lead in a prayer of thanksgiving for the goodness of God that people have experienced.

Bible talk

In the first Bible reading in this service, King David, who probably wrote it, was recognising just how good God was in keeping him safe when he was in danger. Explain how often David found himself in trouble, whether it was facing a huge giant on the battlefield; serving King Saul; knowing that sometimes King Saul might attack him in a fit of madness; or fighting to establish himself as king. God showed how good and kind he was by keeping David safe. God also helped David to do the good and right thing. For example, at one point he could have killed King Saul, his enemy, but he refused to do that. That's why David could write: Taste and see that the Lord is good.

When Jesus was alive on earth, he also showed people just how good and kind God is, for he was God as a human being. He also showed that it mattered about doing what was right and good. Let's explore the story we heard about when Jesus was in the synagogue. (At this point you could show the drama called The Good News on the next page. This is a drama that requires four actors – a newsreader, the woman with a bent back, a reporter and a rabbi. If you use the drama, you will need to include the application points at the end of the presentation printed below.)

Jesus was often to be found speaking with people in the synagogue. Everyone flocked to hear him. We know that sometimes he looked out on a crowd of people listening to him and he was filled with compassion for them. He knew when people were hungry and so he fed them. He knew when people were lost, without anyone to guide them. On this day he looked out over his audience and…(At this point, gaze out over the congregation. Sitting towards the back is a poor woman, with a walking stick, who bends forward and looks down as the leader surveys the crowd. *She will need to be prepared in advance.*) Jesus saw a woman who needed to know just how good God is. She had a spirit inside her, something that was the complete opposite of the goodness of Jesus. (*The woman begins to shuffle forward, very bent over. She might need someone to bring her to the front because she cannot see where to go. Pause dramatically until she gets to the front.*)

This woman was deeply sad inside. She had been bent and twisted for 18 years. (*Ask anyone who is 18 to stand up.*) For the length of this person's life, she had been like this.

- She may have been in pain.
- She struggled to do normal jobs that people have to do, such as putting the washing on the line. (*To demonstrate this, ask the bent woman to stretch up, but she cannot. You may need to get down on your knees to talk with her. You could call some children to the front and ask them to try to do tasks that prove impossible with a bent back – such as walking up some steps, stretching up, running fast, doing up your shoelace, sitting down.*)
- She could not look people in the eyes. Imagine not being able to look at people.
- She was angry inside.

Jesus looked at her and he cared for her. His goodness welled up inside him. He was going to do what was good. He put his hands upon her and said, 'You are now well!' (*The woman straightens up immediately and jigs around in shock and joy! She goes back to her seat.*)

The goodness of Jesus was far stronger than the spirit in this woman and she was healed. Explain that we are not quite sure what is meant by the 'spirit' but we do know that Jesus' goodness and love were able to overcome it. Wow!

But not everyone was happy about this miracle. The leader of the synagogue was deeply unhappy. He did not see the goodness of God in Jesus. He did not think Jesus had done the right thing. Instead he complained that he was breaking the Law. He said that Jesus should not have healed on a Saturday, the Sabbath Day, the day of rest. He was just finding excuses because he did not believe in Jesus.

God is good all the time, but we may not be looking out for his goodness, or we may refuse to acknowledge it when we see or experience him. We may not see his kindness. We may not admit to the rightness of what he does. On this Mothers' Day remind parents that they need to show their children how God wants us to live good and right lives. Lives that please him – the ultimate source of goodness.

In advance ask someone to speak about how they have experienced God's goodness, using language everyone can understand. It might be in healing, or an answer to prayer, or seeing something beautiful in creation, or a new birth, or experiencing God's guidance. They may also be able to point to how they, or someone they know, refused to see God's goodness. (You will need to make it clear to the person how their story fits into the teaching of this outline.)

Drama Script: The Good News

You will need four keen, confident actors. It could be performed live or videoed and shown as a short film.
Characters
Newsreader (NR) – can read from the script as if delivering the news, looking into an imaginary camera.
Nathaniel Daniel (ND) – the roving reporter who interviews Sharon, the healed woman.
Sharon (S) – the woman healed by Jesus.
Rabbi (R) – leader of the synagogue

NR: (*Sitting down behind a table/news desk, looking in to an imaginary camera.*)

And that's almost it from *News 4 Jews*, but before we go we have a good news story for you! Earlier on today, there were reports of a remarkable miraculous incident, this time in Judea. That's right folks, you guessed it, Jesus made another appearance! Earlier this month we reported a miraculous incident in Nain, when Jesus allegedly raised a young man from death to life, to the delight of his grieving, widowed mother! Well, today we've received reports of a healing at the synagogue, so we sent our roving reporter, Nathaniel Daniel, to the scene to find out more…

ND: They say that you come to expect the unexpected in my job, but I can honestly say that I was totally unprepared for the call I received this morning informing me that there were reports of yet another healing – on the Sabbath! As you all know, nothing ever happens on the Sabbath. Nothing is allowed to happen on the Sabbath (unless you're in the entertainment or religion industries of course!) Well, the rumours, it seems, were true, and I have standing with me a remarkable woman with a remarkable story to tell. Sharon, please tell everyone at home what happened to you today.

S: Well, I went to the synagogue and as usual was sitting with the other women. I say 'sit' but actually that was impossible for me with my condition – I could only stand, bent over, leaning against a wall for support.

ND: And why was that, Sharon?

S: Well, I've had terrible back problems which left me crippled with pain and doubled over. I've been staring at people's dusty feet for almost 18 years!

ND: So what's happened today to change that?

S: The girls were all gossiping, saying that Jesus was in town, so I was a bit distracted during the service. You can imagine my surprise when my sister-in-law nudged me and said, 'Sharon, he's calling you over!' and I said, 'Who's calling me? What are you talking about?' 'Jesus!' she said in a loud whisper. And she dragged me over to the front. I couldn't see his face mind you. I was all hunched over. But I could hear his voice…

ND: What did he say?

S: It was something like, and don't quote me on this, 'Woman, you are set free from your pain.' And while I was standing there trying to get my head round what on earth was going on, he put his hands on me. Then I felt (Pause.) … power, that's it, power surging through my body. I thought I was going to keel over but instead the opposite happened and I stood up straight – straight and strong!

ND: What was the first thought that went through your head, Sharon?

S: I think my mind went blank, but then when I got my voice back. I think I said, 'Praise God!' or something like that…

ND: Is this an answer to your prayers, Sharon?

S: Well, yes and no really. For a long time I have asked God to heal me, but as the years went by and nothing happened, I guess I must have stopped praying. I just accepted that it was always going to be like that. In fact I expected it to get worse – not better!

ND: How do you feel now, Sharon?

S: I feel strong. And I'm seeing people's faces for the first time in all these years. For a long time my only view of the world was of the dirt and people's dusty feet. After a while you start to feel like you're not good enough to stand tall and look into people's eyes. Now I feel tall and strong. Jesus called me a 'daughter of Abraham' you know!

ND: We have another eyewitness with us, the synagogue ruler Rabbi David. Rabbi, this is a wonderful story. How do you feel about it happening in your synagogue?

R: Deeply troubled.

ND: I'm sorry? I don't think I heard you correctly.

R: I said, I feel deeply troubled by today's events. If this man Jesus had any respect for the Law, he would have restrained himself and this would have happened on another day in the week, not the Sabbath.

ND: Oh, I see. But surely, Rabbi, this was a good thing – a blessing in fact!

R: Rules are rules.

ND: Right, well… the people of Judea may beg to differ, Rabbi. Word has it that they are delighted with Jesus and all that he is doing in the region. The final word should, of course, go to Sharon. Is there anything you would like to say, Sharon?

S: *(Takes hold of microphone and looks directly at camera.)* If you're watching Jesus, thank you. Thank you so much. I can't tell you what this means to me to be free of the pain. But most of all, to be able to stand tall and look at people face to face. You are good. Thank you… *(Pause.)*

ND: Well, it was a good day in Judea – a good Sabbath – and there are many people here tonight thanking God for Jesus. Nathaniel Daniel reporting for *News 4 Jews.*

Prayers of confession

Remind people of the response of the leader of the synagogue, who did not see God's goodness in the healing of the woman. He did not think Jesus had done what was right. Explain that sometimes we also fail to see God's goodness. We don't always respond with gratitude to God. We may even think he has done the wrong thing if something has gone wrong in our lives. Invite everyone to think back over the last week to the times when they may not have noticed God's goodness.

Have they complained to God because something has not quite gone their way? *(Hold up a miserable face.)*
Has someone been kind to them but they were not grateful? *(Hold up an image of a smiling face.)*
Have they walked by anything that God made and not noticed? *(Hold up a flower or a picture of something in the natural world in your community.)*

Lead a time of confession with this prayer while people keep their eyes open:

Father God, the source of all goodness, we are sorry when, like the leader in the synagogue, we fail to see that what you are doing in our lives is the right thing. *(Hold up the miserable face)*
We are sorry for times when we have not appreciated the love and kindness of those around us, especially those in our family. *(Hold up the smiling face)*
Forgive us for the times when we have not noticed the beauty of your world. *(Hold up the picture from nature)*
For all these things, we are sorry. Please forgive us. Amen.

Response

Prepare a large card mobile phone with an especially large screen. Hand out Post-it notes and pens or pencils.

If someone gives us a present we want to thank them, by letter, email, phone, seeing them or maybe a text. Today we are going to thank God by text. On the Post-it note write a short message to God to thank him or to tell him what we think of him. It can be in a full sentence, a shortened sentence or even a picture. For example:
Thanx gd 4 helpin me with test on fri. u r gr8

Allow five minutes for this, then ask people to bring their text to stick on the screen of the mobile phone at the front.

Prayers of intercession

Good God, we thank you that you are the source of all goodness. We thank you for our mums and dads and carers who demonstrate your goodness to us.
(In silence ask people to thank God for their families.)

Good God, we thank you that you always do what is good and right.

(Pray for somewhere in the world where there is trouble and God's goodness and rightness need to be seen.)

We thank you for the fellowship and encouragement we receive from our church community and the stories we share with each other of your goodness.
Amen.

God's blessing

As a visual, sensory demonstration of God's goodness and his good gifts to us, pass round a basket of chocolates or fruit, inviting everyone to take one. Mums can take two! As the basket is being passed round, explain that this is just one example of God's good gifts to us – which we receive with thanks.

Good Friday

APRIL Psalm 22:1–8,16–18; Luke 23:32–49

Background

The events of Good Friday are very difficult to relate to an all-age congregation, yet vital to our understanding of the Christian message. It is horribly gruesome, so care should be taking in relating the details to a younger audience. But downplaying the reality of the cross robs the event of its power and the cost of the sacrifice Christ made of himself, as well as the measures needed to be taken to enable forgiveness of sin.

This outline focuses on the criminals either side of the crucified Christ, and on their reaction to the death of Jesus. One is self-centred and self-righteous; the other is penitent and recognises Christ for who he is. These criminals reflect the two basic ways people react to the cross – either failing to see that Jesus' death has relevance with personal implications, or else recognising personal sin, the need to respond and the apparent injustice that has been unfairly placed onto an innocent Christ.

In preparation for this service, you are recommended to read *Top Tips: Explaining the cross* (SU) 2008, an easily accessible, essential book for anyone wanting to help children and young people (and adults) understand better the event and the meaning of Jesus' death and resurrection. For more details see page 53.

This outline offers multi-sensory suggestions. The congregation will be able to engage at a level which is right for each person. Younger members will connect with concrete activities and the outline deliberately uses strong visuals and drama to help them stay in touch with the ideas and narrative. There are deeper questions and ideas developed for older people to think and reflect upon.

 **Link**

Users of Scripture Union's *Light* curriculum material in April 2009 will have been exploring God's authority as seen in Mark's account of Jesus' journey through Jericho to Jerusalem, culminating in his death.

Introduction

Prepare a 'lucky dip' bag that contains: a speed limit sign (download and print one from the Internet); a piece of paper with 3/10 and a red cross (wrong) beside it; an Easter egg; a duster. Ensure that these can be seen from the back row.

Ask some children to pull one item each from the bag. Link each one to the following questions, asking if it is fair or unfair that you aren't allowed to:
Speed limit sign: drive as fast as you want on the motorway.
Piece of paper: cheat in tests and exams.
Easter egg: eat all your Easter eggs in one go.
A duster: leave your bedroom untidy.

Each time, after the decision of fair or unfair has been reached, ask if there is another way of looking at the situation. Is there a bigger picture? For example, you aren't allowed to drive as fast as you want because you might kill or injure someone; if you cheated at tests you might not bother to learn anything and it is dishonest; you would get sick if you ate all your Easter eggs in one go; if you didn't tidy your room you might break something that was important to you or might not be able to find something important. Encourage everyone to come up with the 'big picture' reasons themselves. Explore other suggestions of what is fair or unfair. Is there another way of looking at it?

Make the point that we sometimes think things are unfair, but there is often a 'bigger picture' that we need to grasp to appreciate that something else more important is going on than just what affects us.

Prayers of thanksgiving

Ask for ideas of ways in which God cares for us by providing for us. You will need: a long piece of lining paper from a local DIY store (held horizontally at the front of the worship space) and marker pens. On the paper write or draw the suggestions. These might include families, food, education, homes.

Once you have a good list, use it for collective praise, beginning with the words:
Lord, we thank you for all the ways you care for us. We thank you for…

Join together in calling out each item on the list.

Reading the Bible

Psalm 22:1–8,16–18
Luke 23:32–49

Before reading Psalm 22, ask listeners to think about how desperate the writer of the psalm is. What could make someone so miserable? Read the account of the crucifixion slowly, pausing in appropriate places.

Praise

Sing together one or more of the following songs:

'I'm special (because God has loved me)'
'From heaven you came'
'Man of sorrows'
'My song is love unknown'
'When I survey the wondrous cross'

'Thank you for saving me'
'He's got the whole world in his hands (I'll fear no evil)'
'On the cross'

If you anticipate visitors, ensure that at least one song is traditional.

Bible talk

You will need: a cheap or old thin flat white bed sheet; some opaque wide tape (duct tape works well); a high intensity light such as a powerful torch, flood/security light, or overhead projector; dark coloured paper or card; white card or stiff paper; pins; three bulldog clips or similar.

In preparation, make a small cut in the middle of the top of the sheet. (This is to help you to tear it at the end of the talk.) On one side of the sheet, using the tape, make two crosses approximately one metre apart, each one forty centimetres high. When held up, the crosses should be high enough to be seen by a congregation. You could attach the sheet to long poles or broom handles to hold it up during the service. Cut three pieces from the white card, large enough to write the words 'Not fair' on one side, and 'Fair' on the other with a thick black marker. These also need to be large enough to be seen by the congregation. Finally, cut from the darker paper a cross of similar size or slightly larger than the tape crosses on the sheet.

Either before the service starts, or during the service, place the light facing the congregation at the front of the worship area, but don't turn it on. Make sure there is enough distance between the light and the sheet so that the light covers the two crosses when switched on. Ideally the area behind the sheet will have the lights turned off, and the area in front of the sheet will have lights on. This strengthens the impact of the shadows of the crosses later in the talk.

In the service you have already explored the ideas of fair and unfair. You will be drawing these ideas together during the talk.

Talk about the holiness of God. Then explain that when the second temple was built in Jerusalem at the time of Ezra, a special curtain was constructed to divide the Holy Place from the Most Holy Place, which was believed to be where God's home was on earth. (This curtain goes back to the original tabernacle.) It was in the Most Holy Place that once a year a priest met with God. You could refer to Zechariah's actions in Luke 1. *Ask two strong adult volunteers, who know what will be happening in the talk, to hold up the sheet so that the tape crosses are on the back, out of sight of the congregation, and in front of the switched-off light. They should hold the curtain taut and as high as possible throughout the talk.*

This curtain was huge and thick. It was there to protect the priests (who were not holy) from the holiness of God. The closest anyone came to God was Moses who, after meeting God face to face, emerged from the tent with a face shining so brightly that he had to cover it with a cloth.

Using pins, attach the paper or card cross to the front of the sheet, positioning it in the middle of the two crosses which are on the back of the sheet.
The cross was a punishment regularly used by the Romans, who were often hard and brutal. Jesus was falsely accused of causing a riot, encouraging people not to pay taxes and claiming to be a king. He had done nothing wrong, he had never even told a lie. Even the centurion who watched him die realised Jesus' innocence (Luke 23:47). He did not deserve to die.

Ask the congregation at this point if they think it was fair or unfair that Jesus should have been killed even though he had done nothing wrong. *Use a bulldog clip to attach one of the three cards, with the word 'unfair' visible, to the sheet above the cross.*

Yet Jesus accepted the judgement of his enemies, the religious authorities and the Roman governor. *Wonder with the congregation how Jesus might have felt. What would he have thought?* He must have been aware of God's big picture, the plan of salvation which was being worked out at that very moment.

Two criminals were crucified with Jesus at the same time, and their reaction to Jesus' death sheds light on our own reactions. *Turn on the light behind the sheet, which will make the taped crosses visible through the cloth, as shadows. Indicate these two crosses.*

On these two crosses, either side of Jesus, two men died because they had broken the rules of the empire. Ask the congregation if it is fair or unfair to be punished for doing something

wrong. *Attach the remaining cards using the bulldog clips above the two crosses, with the word 'fair' visible.*

Indicate the cross on the left. One of the criminals felt that it was unfair that he should be punished for his own crime. He joined in sneering at Jesus, echoing the tone of Psalm 22 in our first reading (verses 7,8). Jesus used the words from Psalm 22:1 to express his utter loneliness as God the Father turned his back on God the Son. Jesus saw the soldiers gambling over his clothes, reflecting Psalm 22 again (verse 18). It appeared unfair, but Jesus accepted this because he was aware of the bigger picture.

Indicate the cross on the right. The second criminal realised that he deserved the punishment he was getting, but that Jesus didn't deserve it (Luke 23:40-41). Jesus helped him see that there was an eternity ahead of him after his death prompting the criminal to say, 'Jesus, remember me when you come into your kingdom' (Luke 23:42). God's forgiveness was available even for the criminal who humbly turned to Jesus at the last moment of his life. This is one way of explaining the significance of the cross. *Ask the congregation if it was fair or unfair that the criminal should be forgiven. Allow people to decide and you should respond accordingly. Wonder if it was right for our own sin to be placed onto Jesus so that like the thief, we are forgiven. Now refer to the cross representing Jesus and ask the same question. Was it fair for Jesus?*

Point out that Jesus was on the cross not because he had been forced there, but because he was *willing* to be there. Ask, does that make Jesus' death fair or not? Ultimately, Jesus took the punishment that we all deserve. Someone had to do that. That was fair.

Comment on the last words Jesus spoke in Luke 23:46. He trusted his father to know what he was doing. He trusted God's big picture. He trusted that his death on the cross would make it possible for everyone, including one of the thieves, to approach God and be in relationship with him. This meant that no longer was there a Holy Place with limited access to God. And there was a sign – it was like the glory of God was finally revealed to people – because at the moment of Jesus' death the great curtain that hung in the temple was torn in two (Luke

23:45). *The two volunteers pull hard and the cloth is ripped into two pieces revealing the light behind. If possible, all the lights in the worship space will* be turned off at this moment leaving the one light visible. Be careful not to dazzle the congregation uncomfortably.

Response

This activity should immediately follow the talk. With the light shining brightly, a reader stands behind the light source with suitable instrumental music playing on a CD player or a simple keyboard accompaniment. The poem below should be read slowly and reflectively:

Sadness, pain.
Each step another, in the direction of the hill.
That hill, long known the end of the journey.
Why?
Could it not have been some other way?
But no. Those thoughts are gone, back in the garden.
And those that saw, and came to listen, now spit, and jeer.

Nails through flesh.
Two others.
One cries out, 'Save yourself, and me!'
The other, 'Remember me!'
Forgiveness.
Then, finally, final breath.
Curtain
In two.
The way is open, it is finished.

Allow some time for the music to continue after the reading for people to be alone with their own thoughts. Turn the light off when you have finished.

Prayers of intercession

Use the two pieces of the sheet from earlier. Fold and position each one so they make the shape of a cross on the floor.

Each member of the congregation will need a piece of kitchen foil approximately 15cm square – hand this out at a suitable point (for example during the singing of a song). Demonstrate how the foil can be moulded into the shape of a nail. The 'nail' should then be held in the palm of the hand. Read the following prayer thoughts. You could put together a PowerPoint of pictures to support the themes mentioned. A version of this can be downloaded from
Good Friday www.scriptureuion.org.uk/light.

After each reflection encourage the congregation to respond with the words,
'Lord, in your mercy, show your fairness.'

As you hold the nail in your hands, think of the pain Jesus suffered on the cross, the unfairness of it all, and yet it was part of God's big picture. Let us think and pray now for those who are in pain, remembering that God is always in control…

Think of others who face an unfair situation through no fault of their own…

Think of those who are homeless, or confused, or feel unloved…

Think of those we know who are sick…

Think of those who are jobless or face an uncertain future…

Think of those who feel life has passed them by…

Sing one or two of the suggested songs gently, whilst the 'nails' are collected and laid on the material. Focus the attention of the congregation on the image created.
Suggested songs:
'I will offer up my life'
'What kind of love is this?'
'Show me the way of the cross (once again)'
'Oh lead me, to the place (Where I can find you)'

Prayers of confession

Explain to the congregation that because of our failure to live as God wants, each one of us is, in a way, responsible for Jesus' death on the cross. Continue by saying this confession, (or say it together from a PowerPoint or OHT slide):

Let the nail that has been given become a symbol of asking God for forgiveness. (Pause.)
Let the nail that has been taken away from us and laid on the cross be a symbol that our sin has been taken away.
It is a symbol that our sin is forgiven.

Conclude by reading Hebrews 10:19–22.

God's blessing

Close the service with the following words of blessing:

By the Father's great and unimaginable love, we are saved.
By the wounds in Jesus' hands, we are healed.
By the power of the Holy Spirit we can faithfully follow.
And so may the Lord of all guide us, strengthen us, and teach us to trust him more today and for ever.
Amen.

Easter Sunday

APRIL Psalm 46; Matthew 28:1–10

Background

We live with the benefit of hindsight! This day, of all days, is our day for joyful celebration – the heart of our 'good news'. On the first Easter, Jesus' closest friends were stunned, amazed and even afraid of what had happened – it was beyond their expectations. The first thing the angel had to say was 'Do not be afraid'. We don't know if the women were afraid because of the earthquake or the angel!

The disciples were (eventually) filled with joy at the resurrection of Jesus. Since we know the whole story, we anticipate the joy, even in the sadness of Good Friday. Today is a day to focus on that joy. Jesus' resurrection vindicated all his claims and is the sign and seal of our hope for resurrection too. We can remind God's people that our hope is secure. We look for the living Jesus in the world of the living. As part of his body, we must be his hands, feet and voice. We share the good news, because it is not for an elite group, but for everyone.

But many believers still live in fear, doubt or confusion. God's messengers constantly tell his people not to be afraid. God reiterates that message through the Psalms and in accounts such as in Joshua 1:6-9. It is through the hard times that our faith is tested and strengthened. This is emphasised in Psalm 46, where all kinds of natural and man-made disasters beset the singers. Yet they hold on to their security in God. Even when everything around us is shifting and changing, we can depend on God. So, today, as we focus on the joy of resurrection and the love demonstrated in sacrifice, let us urge each other to live fully the life Jesus came to offer and not live in fear.

You are strongly recommended to read *Top Tips: Explaining the cross* (SU) 2008 – an easily accessible essential book for anyone wanting to help children and young people (and adults) understand better the event and the meaning of Jesus' death and resurrection. See page 53 for details.

The aim of this outline is to help each person present to examine how the resurrection affects basic attitudes and feelings; that God's love and faithfulness can remove crippling doubts and fears; that his presence gives joy whilst his call on our lives gives purpose.

 **Link**

Users of Scripture Union's *Light* curriculum material in April 2009 are in the middle of exploring God's authority which is given ultimate expression in Jesus' triumph over death in the resurrection.

Introduction

You will need a lidded box tied up with ribbon, with a £10 note Blu-tacked inside the lid; a piggy bank containing foreign coins, washers and nails; a model or picture of the tomb at sunrise.

Making a great show, invite people to suggest what might be in the box. After some ideas, someone can come to open the box. Ask how they feel (and how everyone feels) to discover that it is empty. (Disappointed, let down, deflated.)

Do something similar with the piggy bank – how much money? Again, explore the feelings when it is not what they expect. (Angry, cheated.)

Then ask about the tomb – how would the women have felt to find it empty? (Confused, upset, afraid.)

Sometimes our initial reactions, whilst natural, are wrong. Show them the hidden £10 note, and give it to the person who opened the box! Ask how hindsight changes our reaction to the empty tomb. What do the congregation feel when they see it? (We will come back to the piggy bank later.)

Reading the Bible

Do this in the 'normal' way for your church – either both readings back to back, or separated by a song or other activity to help people reflect for themselves on what was read.

Psalm 46
Matthew 28:1–10

Ask one person in advance to read Psalm 46. Ensure they can read with varied pitch and volume to contrast the tumult with the calm presence of God.

Ask three people in advance to read the Matthew passage with a narrator, an angel and Jesus. Suggest to the congregation that they listen out for three key phrases said by the angel and Jesus:
'Don't be afraid!'
'He is not here!'
'Go and tell!'

Praise

Use PowerPoint, OHT or a printed service order to share this liturgy, updating Psalm 136. It is available on the website as a download **Easter** www.scriptureunion.org.uk/light. Put the congregation into two groups, and read antiphonally. Note the change in those reading the refrain, for the sake of variety!

Give thanks to God whose power existed before time began
His love has no expiry date
Who spun the universe into place, galaxy by galaxy
His love has no expiry date
Who gave us a beautiful planet
His love has no expiry date
He rescued his people Israel
His love has no expiry date.

God gave them judges and kings
His love has no expiry date
He loves us as a precious treasure
His love has no expiry date
And gave us Jesus to live as our example
His love has no expiry date
Jesus showed us obedience
His love has no expiry date
Obedience even to death
His love has no expiry date.

Jesus paid the price of our ransom
His love has no expiry date
And took the punishment we were due
His love has no expiry date
He shone as a light to the nations
His love has no expiry date
And called Gentiles to follow God

His love has no expiry date
He made us part of his family
His love has no expiry date
A holy nation of royal priests
His love has no expiry date.

God sent his Spirit to guide us
His love has no expiry date
To be our comfort and our strength
His love has no expiry date.

He heals us in and out
His love has no expiry date
And shelters us in times of trouble
His love has no expiry date
He has called us upward to heaven
His love has no expiry date.

And we will see him face to face
His love has no expiry date
Oh give thanks to God our Saviour
His love has no expiry date.

Bible talk

As people enter church, they should be given a 'face' that is happy on one side and sad on the other, or be asked to draw a happy face on one hand and a sad face on the other. (This could be done using non-toxic felt-tips left at the end of each pew or row of chairs).

Invite everyone to think about the feelings evoked by today's Bible readings. They should indicate their feelings or those of the people in the stories using their 'face' or hands. If necessary, encourage people by acknowledging what they show. You could encourage interaction by showing 'faces' on your own hands, especially if you naturally gesture a lot when you speak. It may be helpful to demonstrate the contrast in feelings to encourage those who are shy about expressing their opinion, even by showing a face.

Ask people to reflect on times of trouble in their own lives and what feelings are evoked or provoked by trouble. Make a specific point of including children. Ask if anyone has actually experienced an earthquake or stormy seas. Let them briefly describe what it was like, what happened and how they felt.

Remind the congregation that the people of Israel experienced times of trouble throughout their history – storms, famines, invasions, war and exile. These are things that make anyone anxious and fearful. Yet, when they were at their best, the people held on to the faithfulness and promises of God. Even in the times of trouble, their confidence and hope was in God and they could experience a joy that was supernatural, not natural. So, Psalm 46 contrasts a natural reaction to fearful situations with a

God-rooted reaction that trusts him. Through natural troubles God's people expected him to be with them, to fill them with joy (verse 4). Even through the man-made disaster of war, the nation of Israel held on to the sovereignty of God and expected him to bring the war to an end. Yet, even as it continued, they could find peace by focusing on knowing what God is like and looking forward to the day when everyone would know and acknowledge God's sovereignty (verse 10).

Now jump forward in your thinking to the first Easter Sunday. Remind everyone of what the disciples might have known about people coming back to life, from the Old Testament and from the life of Jesus – after the prayers of Elijah and of Elisha (this is especially relevant if you have used the first outline on Elisha in this book); after Lazarus was raised from death; remembering what they had heard Jesus say about his death and resurrection. But his disciples were not expecting Jesus to come alive again. They were like us with the piggy bank – the contents were not what anyone expected. They thought the Messiah would be a warrior and throw the Romans out of Israel. They were deflated, disappointed and grieving.

(Use the three phrases from the reading of Matthew as much as you can in the following narrative.) Ask people to imagine themselves arriving at the tomb with the women, to finish embalming the body. They were so sad. And the tomb was empty. How would they have felt? Suddenly, an angel spoke! As usual, the first thing the angel said was, '**Don't be afraid**'! What does that show about how the women might have been feeling? The normal reaction in the Bible to meeting an angel is to be afraid; many people, like the guards here, fell fainting to the floor! No wonder angels always say, '**Don't be afraid**'. Meeting God's messenger fills people with fear because they expect a word of judgement.

Point out that a message about judgement is not what the angel was trying to pass on here. The angel reminded them of what Jesus had said and showed them the empty tomb. He stated the obvious, '**He isn't here**'. He did not tell them where Jesus was. (In Luke's Gospel, the angel says, 'Why do you look for the living among the dead?') Wow! How must the women have felt? They came to grieve over a dead friend and then discovered not only was he not there, but he was no longer dead!

Despite this mind-blowing information, the angel has not finished. He gave them the task to '**Go and tell the disciples**'. How must the women have felt about this? They became God's messengers at a time when Jewish men never listened to what women said and when women couldn't act as witnesses in court!

That morning must have been an emotional rollercoaster.

Notice that even as they gladly turned away, they were still scared. But their joy was complete when they met Jesus. They touched him and they worshipped him. And what did he say? '**Don't be afraid! Go and tell!**' The resurrection of Jesus was a 'once only' event. He would never grow old, never die again. He had defeated fear and death… So, today, as we remember and celebrate the resurrection, how does that make us feel?

Challenge everyone, saying something similar to this: Listen again to these three key phrases, '**Don't be afraid!**'; '**He is not here!**'; '**Go and tell!**' When you go from here today, let those phrases direct where you go and what you do. Begin the next day of your joy-filled, fear-free resurrection life now!

Make sure that everyone understands that 'He is not here!' means 'Jesus is not dead'. You don't want anyone to think that God is not here with us any more!

Prayers of confession

You will need a whiteboard (on an easel or free-standing) covered in red whiteboard pen, plus a number of red whiteboard pens. The easel should be hidden or turned away from the congregation.

Ask the congregation what happens if you mix red paint with red paint, or red light with red light. (Stays red.) Remind them that Isaiah says that our scarlet sins will be white as snow (Isaiah 1:18). The cross gives us an example where red plus red makes white! (sins plus blood equals forgiveness).

Remind everyone that we all think, say and do things that are wrong. Or we sometimes don't think, say or do something we should. These wrong things can mean that we fail to trust God. We are fearful. The wrong things we do can lead us to doubt that God is with us or they can mean that we don't share Jesus' good news with others. However, if we are sorry, Jesus will forgive us for our lack of trust, doubt and disobedience. Give everyone a chance to think of things they would like to say sorry for:

for when they have not trusted God and been afraid; for when they have doubted God is there; for when they have not shared the good news of Jesus with others.

Bring out the whiteboard or turn it round. The red stands for all the wrong that we do or say or the right that we don't do. Explain that writing on the red with red whiteboard pen takes the red away – red plus red makes white! To show that people are sorry, they can come and write their name on the board. It does not matter if the names all cross over each other. This 'making white' symbolises their forgiveness. You may wish to play quiet music as people come forward. Close the time with a prayer like this:

Father, thank you for sending Jesus to take away our wrongdoing.
We are sorry that every day we do things that let you down.
Thank you that you do forgive us and take away our fear.
Fill us with your joy. Amen.

Prayers of thanksgiving

This could be an appropriate time for singing. Suitable songs might include:

'Thank you for the cross'
'Thank you for saving me'
'Thank you, thank you for the blood that you shed'
'God's not dead!'
'The price is paid'

'All my days'
'Joyful, joyful'

If you have a really good choir, they might sing 'Jesu, Joy of Man's Desiring' as an anthem, while the congregation think about all the good things we have because Jesus lived, died and rose again.

Prayers of intercession ~Recorded music.~

You will need to set up three prayer 'stations':

Invite the congregation to think first about themselves – what they are afraid of, in what ways they are not open to God or where they have not shared Jesus with others. Then ask them to think more widely about others. Who do they know who is afraid? Who lives in situations where God seems to be absent? Who can they think of who has never had a chance to hear about Jesus?

Ask everyone to move around the prayer stations offering prayers for both themselves and others.

Don't be afraid – with heart-shaped cards for people to take away after they have prayed; pens; heart-shaped plastic jewels. Here people write their own name or that of a friend onto the heart, then add a phrase such as 'Take away my fear' on the other side. They can take that or a plastic jewel heart to symbolise their prayer.

He is not here – with a blank sheet of paper; a map of the world; Post-it notes and pens. Here people can use the Post-it note either to name areas of their life where they would like to be more open to God, or to write names of places, nearby or overseas, where people need to know that God is there. They can place the note either on the blank sheet or on the appropriate part of the map.

Go and tell – with photos, cards or aid leaflets with pictures of people local, national and international. Also, tea lights (suitably placed) and matches or tapers. (This needs careful supervision.) Here people can light a tea light to symbolise a desire to tell others or share by their lives that Jesus is alive among family, friends and neighbours. They may then ask God to shine his light in situations where darkness seems to be 'winning'. They may be prompted to pray for people or places identified in the pictures, cards and leaflets.

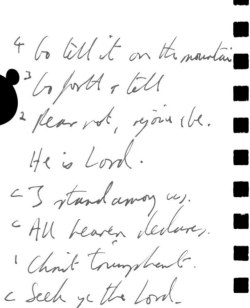

(Handwritten annotations in margins:) ~Main~ ~E+S~ ~Font.~ ~MM.~ ~N. Ande~ ~Sue~

(Handwritten list, lower right:)
~4 Go tell it on the mountain~
~3 Go forth + tell~
~2 Fear not, rejoice etc.~
~He is Lord.~
~← 3 stand among us.~
~← All heaven declares.~
~1 Christ triumphant.~
~← Seek ye the Lord.~

Response ✓

Stand with hands joined in rows or groups. Pray this prayer, joining together in the refrain:

O living God,
Help us to share with others the joy and hope of your resurrection.
Lord, fill us with your joy!
Help us to shine your light into the dark places where people are in fear or danger, here and abroad.

Lord, fill us with your joy!
Help us to serve others with gentleness and humility, so we tell others about your love, grace and mercy.
Lord, fill us with your joy!
Help us to live in the fullness of the life you came to give.
Amen.

God's blessing

Close your service using this prayer, or something similar:

Heavenly Father, bless us with the light of your presence.
Living Son, bless us with the peace beyond understanding.
Blazing Spirit, bless us with the power to live wisely.
And on this day of all days, grant us the joy of hope secured in your resurrection.
Amen.

Pentecost

MAY Joel 2:28–32; Acts 2:1–39

TRANSFORMING POWER

Background

Imagine the scene. The disciples and all the other followers of Jesus are in the same place in Jerusalem. They are waiting. Waiting for the promise given by Jesus before he died (see John 14:15–26 and 16:4–15). Jesus gave this promise again during those amazing 40 days after his death when he 'gave many convincing proofs that he was alive' (Acts 1:3). Suddenly, with the city heaving with devout Jews from far and wide, the promise is fulfilled. It becomes reality and changes the disciples' lives for ever. The Spirit enables them to do things they have never done before – speak foreign languages, speak in front of a large crowd and, later, to heal people and explain the Scriptures. People listening are moved to repentance and commitment to God, by the Spirit. How exciting for the followers and everyone present at that first Pentecost – and how exciting for us! Not only was the Spirit sent to help and work in the lives of Jesus' disciples, but he also is active in our lives today.

Whatever your churchmanship, Pentecost is a crucially important date in the church calendar, as it is vital to see the coming of the Holy Spirit within God's big plan for salvation. The Spirit is present in the Old Testament, but his role is not often in evidence. But when the promised helper (John 14:15–26 and 16:4–15) arrives, there is a remarkable transformation. There are countless stories of the transforming power of God's Spirit since then until the present day.

As you celebrate Pentecost, try to engender some of the excitement of that first day when the followers experienced the power of the Spirit and also the excitement of what God wants to do through the Spirit in our own lives. The Holy Spirit is God everywhere, always ready to help, comfort, counsel, guide and correct. What a privilege to live our lives with the Spirit! In the power of the Spirit we have been entrusted with the privilege of telling others about God, just as Peter did on the first Pentecost.

 **Link**

In May 2009, users of Scripture Union's *Light* curriculum material have been focusing on God living with his people through the life of Jacob. When the Spirit came at Pentecost, God came to live with his people in a new way. The two passages in this outline are the same as those in the *Light* material.

Introduction

To introduce the theme of transformation, show the congregation a clip of a film where an obvious transformation takes place. There are plenty of examples, but here are some suggestions which are all U-rated,
In *Shrek*, show an extract where Fiona transforms from a woman into an ogre.
In *Shrek 2*, choose the scene where Donkey is transformed into a stallion.
In *Bee Movie*, show the clip where pollen is once again distributed over Central Park.

Before you show the clip, encourage the congregation to see what has been transformed. This should be easy! After the clip, talk about how easy it was to spot the transformation from the film. There was nothing hidden, it was obvious what changes had taken place. Now ask everyone to think about other transformations in their lives. If your church is comfortable doing so, ask people to chat in pairs, groups or families about those transformations. Ask them to remember these for later in the service.

If your church does not have film-playing facilities you could ask someone to describe what happens to Fiona in *Shrek*, or bring in a Transformer robot to demonstrate how it changes into a car. Or even discuss what happens to Cinderella and her coach at midnight!

Explain that today is Pentecost, the time when God sent the Holy Spirit to be with everyone who followed him. He transformed, beyond recognition, the lives of those who were present with Jesus at that time.

Praise

Sing together songs which speak of the Holy Spirit. Make sure you have a good mix of upbeat and more reflective songs, so that people have a chance to sing songs which help them to worship God. Here are some suggestions:

'As we lift up your name'
'There must be more'
'Down the mountain the river flows'

If you have the facilities, you could project pictures traditionally associated with the Holy Spirit – a dove, flames and wind (or the effects of wind) – to help people who appreciate visual stimuli to engage with the words of the songs. You could encourage people to use flags and ribbons as they praise God. Be aware though that, for some people, this kind of worship is more of a distraction than another way of praise, so be sensitive to the different needs of people in the church. This is a joyous time and it would be a shame for anything to spoil the service for some members of the congregation!

Old & New 611   Spirit of God (3v)

The Spirit lives to set us free (1st+last).
O holy Spirit
Spirit of the living God.

I hear the sound
O thou who camest
Spirit of holiness.

61

Reading the Bible

Joel 2:28–32 — *1 reader*
Acts 2:1–39 — *2 readers*

You could just read the Joel passage as it is, but it does form the words to a song from the musical *Saints Alive!* by Roger Jones. As an alternative to reading the passage, get hold of a recording and play it to the congregation, putting the words of the passage on PowerPoint or OHP acetate.

Use this combination of reading and retelling to help the congregation explore the passage from Acts 2. You will need two readers.

Read Acts 2:1–4.

Retell Acts 2:5–13: There were Jews from all over the world in Jerusalem that day – from east and west, from north and south. When they each heard one of the followers talking in their language they were surprised. But they were more than just surprised. They were totally confused. They were listening to the great things God had done, in their own language. Some of them wanted to know what that meant. But others were sceptical: 'They're drunk!' they shouted.

Read Acts 2:14–15.

Retell Acts 2:22–36: Peter carried on telling the crowd all about Jesus, and that what was happening had been predicted by the prophet, Joel, as we heard in the last reading. He told them, 'You took Jesus and had him nailed to a cross. But this was all part of God's plan. King David knew what would happen hundreds of years ago! He said so in the Psalms. Jesus is in heaven right now, and has sent us his Holy Spirit – that's what you're seeing and hearing! Everyone should know: Jesus is Lord and Christ!'

Read Acts 2:37–39.

Alternatively omit the second reading and use the drama sketch below to tell the story.

Bible talk

Remind the congregation about the transformation they saw at the start of the service. What was it that made the transformation possible? Talk about the power behind the change in the clip you saw.

Turn to the Bible passages you have just heard. First, in the Joel prophecy, ask what changes he talked about and what would bring them about? (If people cannot remember, show them the passage on an acetate or PowerPoint. Emphasise the fact that it was the Spirit who would make this happen.)

Explain that Joel was a prophet who was speaking to the people of Israel at a time when their land had been destroyed by locusts. He declared that the locusts were punishment for all the bad stuff that Israel had done. But if they would only turn back to God, he would rescue them and bless them greatly in the way that is described here. Their lives would be transformed from desperation to hope and blessing!

Move on to the Acts passage and either use this script or recap on what happened.

Introduce a member of the congregation dressed up like Peter (either in a first-century costume, or a modern outfit that reflects Peter's character).

Leader (L): Peter! Great to see you! You've had quite an experience – tell us all about it!
Peter (P): Well, where shall I start? It's all been fantastic!
L: Begin at the beginning.
P: OK, so in the beginning, God created the heavens and the earth…
L: No, not that far back. I meant the beginning of your day.
P: (*Laughs.*) I've just spent ages talking to the crowds, so my tongue is running away with me

a bit! (*Pauses to get thoughts together.*) How long have I got? There's so much that I want to say!

L: Tell us what set it all off.

P: Well, it was Jesus, really. We'd been with him for three years, travelling around, listening to his teaching, watching him heal people and help them get right with God. And then he was killed. And we were so scared. (*Pauses.*) You know that he was killed, don't you, and came back to life again?

L: Yes, I've heard about that!

P: So, just before he died, he said that he was going away, but that he would send a helper in his place. He was with us for 40 days after he came back to life and then he went to heaven. Just before he went, he told us again to wait around until this helper came.

L: So, who is this helper?

P: He's the Holy Spirit! He comes from God and is God – he is God everywhere!

L: So how did he come? Did he just knock on your door and say 'Hi'?

P: Not exactly! All of the followers of Jesus were waiting together in the upstairs room where we usually meet. Suddenly there was a really loud noise, one like a rushing wind. All around us, there were these quiverings of fire. I'm not sure how you'd describe them! Like moving ribbons of fire. Tongues even! They swept through the room, and then touched us all – but we didn't catch alight! It was scary, but reeeeally exciting!

L: So what was this 'fire'?

P: It was the Holy Spirit touching us, like fire, and almost overwhelming us. We started speaking foreign languages – Median, Persian, Latin, Greek – and none of us had ever been to language school! We ran out into the street and a crowd gathered. There were people from all over the world in Jerusalem, and each one of them heard one of us speaking about the wonderful things God has done, in their own language. What a way to tell people about Jesus!

L: What did the people you met think?

P: Some of them were amazed and confused at the same time. But other people thought we were drunk! Imagine that! The cheek of it! It was only nine o'clock in the morning! So I told the crowd what had happened – who Jesus was, that he had died and come back to life. I told them what God had promised in Joel – I think I heard you reading that passage earlier on – and that it had all come true! 'Turn back to God!' I said – and thousands did. Thousands believed that God had raised Jesus from the dead!

L: That's amazing! What are you going to do now?

P: We can't go on waiting – the promised helper has arrived. We could sit around, hiding away in our homes like we did before. But we've got to get out there and tell people about Jesus. The Holy Spirit is here to help us do just that! Right now! (*Peter runs off.*)

Talk about the change that the Holy Spirit brought about in the lives of Jesus' followers. Retell some of the great things the followers went on to do: the healing of the lame man (Acts 3), Philip and the Ethiopian official (Acts 8), Peter healing Dorcas and Aeneas (Acts 9).

Comment on the differences between the followers of Jesus before the Spirit came (scared, unsure, timid) and after (bold, brave, certain). The Spirit enabled them to heal the sick, raise dead people, speak different languages and explain the Scriptures. What a transformation!

Prayers of thanksgiving

Before the service, ask someone in your congregation to speak about a time when the Holy Spirit was responsible for a transformation in their lives. (It might be easier for everyone to identify with the idea of transformation if they hear of a specific example of someone known to them. Encourage this person to speak in jargon-free language!) They may be someone who has kicked a bad habit through the Holy Spirit, or someone whose conversion owed a lot to a dramatic change brought about by the Spirit. A child might have known Jesus with them by his Spirit in a challenging situation. Interview the person, asking them to outline briefly this transformation and how the interviewee was thankful for the transforming power of the Holy Spirit!

If appropriate, give a chance for others in small groups to share any changes brought about by the Spirit, with reference to any discussion in the 'Introduction' to this service. Comment on the different transformations, big and small, that the Holy Spirit can make.

Read Jesus' words in John 16:8–15 about the Spirit and draw out the different roles he plays – showing up sin for what it is, guiding us to the truth in Jesus and transforming us to be more like him! Finish with a prayer thanking God for the Spirit and the transformations you have discussed.

Prayers of confession

Sometimes we can resist the work of the Spirit, because we don't want to respond to the challenge of the Spirit or don't want to acknowledge him in our lives. Ask what might have happened if the followers of Jesus had kept everything to themselves, remained full of fear and refused to proclaim boldly the good news of Jesus. This is a speculative discussion but is something that many will not have thought of.

Ask the congregation to come before God to say sorry for the times they have resisted God's transforming Spirit and refused to recognise wrongdoing. Everyone joins in the refrain of this prayer. Pause after each sentence:

Spirit of God, sometimes I block up my ears and refuse to listen to you when you show me where I have done or said or thought something wrong.
I'm sorry.
Spirit of God, sometimes I close my eyes so that I cannot see where there is injustice in the world or where I need to get involved to make a difference.
I'm sorry.
Spirit of God, sometimes I forget about your power and strength and make my weakness an excuse for not telling others about Jesus.

I'm sorry.
Spirit of God, sometimes I don't want to change to become more like Jesus. It makes me feel uncomfortable.
I'm sorry.
Spirit of God, please forgive me and transform me.
Amen.

On different pieces of paper, display the words 'I'm sorry' in different languages. Stick these around the building. Encourage people to move around, stopping at each piece of paper and asking God by his Spirit to forgive them for the wrong the Spirit has just shown them. Alternatively, people could move from one 'I'm sorry' to another after each of the prayers above.

Here are some examples, but if you have people who can speak a different language, ask them for other translations:

Je suis desolé (French)
Lo siento (Spanish)
Omlouvam se (Czech)
Ik ben droevig (Dutch)
Jeg er trist (Norwegian)
Mujhe muaf kr dai (Urdu)
Es tut mir leid (German).

Response

Praise God together, singing songs which speak of being transformed, such as:

'Who is there like you?'
'Search my soul'

Then sing songs which affirm our commitment to speak of God's transforming Spirit to others in the world:

'The Spirit of the Lord'
'They that wait'
'Father of creation'

Try to engender a feeling of excitement about being changed by the Spirit. Read Acts 2:38,39, emphasising how life-changing the coming of the Spirit was, not only for Jesus' followers but for the people who heard them!

Prayers of intercession

Hymns Old + New 932

As your musician(s) continues to play one of the songs from 'Response', ask the congregation to think about someone they know who needs to hear about the transforming Spirit of God. Give out pens and flame shapes, cut from yellow, red and orange paper, and ask everyone to write down the name of the person in their mind. Place a large sheet of paper (a piece of old wallpaper is ideal) at the front of the church and ask everyone to stick their flame to the paper. Sing once again, being mindful of the people on the 'flames', and finish with a prayer, thanking God for the Spirit. Pray that as you talk to these people about Jesus, God will give you all the same courage and excitement that Peter had.

After the service, position your fire somewhere where it will be seen, and ask everyone to carry on praying for these people over the next few weeks.

God's blessing

Recap on what you have learnt during the service – that the Spirit of God came to the followers of Jesus which brought about a huge transformation – both in Jesus' followers themselves and in the people who heard them speaking. Remind everyone of the continuing transforming power of the Spirit, as seen in the life of the person interviewed earlier.

Conclude with this prayer:

May God the Spirit empower and transform you.
May God the Son inspire you to follow him.
May God the Father surround you with his love.
Amen.

Intercession Thanksgiving.

Ribbons circulate at signing

Then gathered + fixed to fan.

Turn on fan to animate prayers

Fathers' Day

JUNE Genesis 22:1–12; Luke 14:25–35

Background

We rightly tend to use Fathers' Day as an opportunity to recognise God as our heavenly Father, and to thank him for the provision of earthly fathers to care for and support their children. In an age when education and example are often seen as the responsibility of government with role models outside the family, it is also important to consider the vital place of Christian fathers (and indeed grandfathers, uncles and for that matter, mothers) in setting an example for younger members of the family. Often it is the actions of parents rather than their words that communicate appropriate priorities and shape lives; as St. Francis of Assisi said: 'Preach the gospel at all times, and if necessary use words.'

Setting a good fatherly example can require discipline, and often a preparedness to do things that we or our family will find unpalatable. There is no finer example of this than that of Abraham, who didn't just affirm God with his words, but was prepared to go as far as sacrificing his son in obedience to God as God tested his faith. It seems unlikely that Isaac ever had cause to doubt his father's commitment to God, having seen it in action! This is a powerful story with an emphasis not on the fact that Abraham might have killed his son (which in our contemporary world may appear shocking), but that he obeyed his God.

Jesus calls us to live lives with God at the forefront. Good parents need to go further than talking about that, they need to model it in their daily lives.

As this is a service for Fathers' Day, make sure that information is available about any men's or dads' ministry that is running or might be launched in the near future.

 **Link**

Users of Scripture Union's *Light* curriculum material have been focusing in June 2009 on God who listens and responds as they explore the life of the early church in Acts 8–12. Abraham listened and responded in complete obedience to the God who himself listens and responds, a suitable parallel to the stories of the early church.

Introduction

To introduce the key concept that our actions demonstrate our priorities and authenticate our beliefs, encourage everyone to play the £100 game as they arrive and settle into their seats. Print out and copy the pdf from

Fathers_1 www.scriptureunion.org.uk/light and give a copy of it and a pencil to everyone or every family unit as they arrive, or leave a copy on each chair for people to complete as they wait for the service to start.

Praise

Sing together one or more of the following songs/hymns:

'Father God I wonder'
'O Jesus I have promised'
'I want to serve the purpose of God'
'All heaven declares'

Introduction (continued)

The £100 game highlights the fact that the choices we make or the things we give up or sacrifice demonstrate the strongest indication of what is important to us and what our priorities are. When people have completed the chart, invite a number of them to share the choices they have made. You could ask for volunteers or warn people in advance. Make sure children are involved.

More graphic than people talking through their choices would be to use some props for people to act them out. To do this you will need to be prepared with the following:

- Either a real bundle of £5 and £10 notes making £100, or slips of paper cut to the appropriate size with denominations written on them.
- A football or football scarf representing the football tickets of the local team.

- Two A4 pieces of paper with 'Admit One' written on them representing cinema tickets.
- Some aluminium foil dishes or chopsticks representing the Chinese meal.
- A pair of shoes, or trainers, or a shoe box
- A CD
- A large bar of chocolate
- A computer game box
- A bottle of wine
- A shirt/blouse on a hanger, or a large carrier bag from a known clothing store.
- A picnic hamper
- A collection box or collection plate to symbolise the donation to the church.

Give the real or pretend notes to the volunteer and invite them to act out their choices by 'buying' items and placing the remaining donation in the collection box/plate.

Prayers of thanksgiving

Psalm 127:3 reminds us that all children are a gift from God. Children and adults are truly blessed if they have people who have been good role models, whether they are parents, friends or mentors. This thanksgiving will encourage those who are parents, grandparents or carers to thank God for their children, and everyone to thank God for the people who have set a special example to them. Hand out blank postcard-sized cards and invite people to write or draw on it the name of someone who is important to them and who has set them a good example. They can also write down, if appropriate, the names of any child(ren) who is (are) important to them.

Everyone holds up their card as you lead a prayer of thanks for children and for those who care for and set a good example to us. The prayer is concluded with everyone holding up their card and saying the following together:

Thank you God for _____. Amen.

This card will be used in the Response at the end of the service.

Reading the Bible

Genesis 22:1–12
Luke 14: 25–35

To bring more realism to the drama of the passage from Genesis, select a father and son to read the parts of Abraham and Isaac, with others taking the part of narrator and the voice of God. If you are using the drama below, you may want to use Genesis 12:1–9 instead or just miss out the Genesis 22 reading. Genesis

12:1–9 sets the scene for what happens to Abraham later, which is seen in the drama.

You may wish to begin the Luke reading at verse 27 if the version you use includes the word 'hate'. It might take some time, and be a distraction, to explain what 'hate' means in the context. The whole passage is about putting God first and what that costs.

Bible talk

The following scripts are provided as a drama for four actors to perform. There are two scenes to be shown one after the other. Both might need a brief introduction. You may choose the same actors as those used in reading the Bible passages. If you feel that the drama is too graphic for your congregation, then either use only the first part or just use the Genesis 22 Bible reading. The application on page 70 will be the same.

Make it clear that the scenes are a dramatisation of the story, and therefore some poetic licence has been used.

The scene is a tent, and inside Sarah is cooking a meal. (If you decide to dress up for the drama

and use props choose a modern-day setting and a kitchen, or a tent and a log fire.)

Sarah (S) looks up in surprise as Abraham (A) enters the tent.

A: Sarah! I'm home!
S: Ah! Abraham, you're back at last. Dinner's going to be twenty minutes. Where's Isaac?
A: Oh, he's just helping the servants feed the donkey.
S: Well it must have been a hard few days, you look exhausted.
A: I'm drained.
S: Can't say I'm surprised. A six day camping trip, at your age. Where was it you went?
A: Moriah.

S: Isn't that the place in the *Lord of the Rings*? Did you see any hobbits?

A: No. Nothing as odd as that!

S: Honestly, what is God doing asking you to go all the way to those mountains just to sacrifice a lamb?

A: (*looking sheepish.*) Well, he didn't actually ask me to go all that way just to sacrifice one lamb.

S: Well how many did he ask you to sacrifice?

A: None.

S: None? You and Isaac and two servants walked six days to sacrifice nothing?

A: Not exactly.

S: What do you mean? What *did* you go for?

A: Well, God asked me to go and sacrifice Isaac.

S: (*Shocked and panicking.*) No! Oh, Abraham. Tell me you didn't do it! Tell me you brought him home!

A: Relax. Relax. He's fine. He's fine.

S: So what happened?

A: Well, God told me to take Isaac off to Moriah and sacrifice him. I think it was to test me, to make sure that I am really obedient to God.

S: After all we've been through? After the time we left your hometown and family to go to some place we didn't know where, or the time you let Lot, your nephew, keep the green, flat plains while you kept to the tough hills in Canaan, or the time when you chased and defeated the kings who took Lot as a prisoner!!

A: Well… yes. But God said go, and even though it sounded nuts, I just have to do whatever he tells me. Let's face it, all that we have been through up to now just would not make sense if I suddenly stopped listening to God.

S: But what doesn't make sense is that God tells you that our descendants will become a whole nation. Then God makes us wait forever to have just one son. Then God tells you to kill that one son. How on earth can you be sure of what he is telling you? How do you know when God is speaking to you?

A: The point is, Sarah, if you spend all your time looking for reasons not to trust what God tells you, then you will always be surrounded by doubts. When I hear God speaking I have to follow. Not question. Follow.

S: Well, that's all very admirable. Very impressive. But what do you think your obedience has done for Isaac? I mean, how do you think he is feeling about the fact that you were going to sacrifice him?

The next scene shows Isaac (I) and one of the servants (Sv) tidying away after their journey. (You might want to provide a coil rope or a blanket to fold as a prop.)

I: Right, that's the donkey fed. Now, time to get some food.

Sv: Yeah, I'm starving.

I: Me too.

Sv: Errm… Isaac?

I: Yes.

Sv: Can I ask you something?

I: Sure. Shoot.

Sv: Well, what went on back there?

I: You just helped me feed the donkey and unpack.

Sv: No. Back there in Moriah, up the mountain.

I: Oh, right. Well it was all a bit weird. When we got to the place where God had told Dad to build the altar, we still didn't have a goat or lamb to put on it as a sacrifice. So I asked Dad what we were going to do, and he said that God would provide something.

Sv: How did he know?

I: Well, one thing I know about Dad is that he has a hotline to God. He's good like that. I mean that was how he knew we had to go to Moriah in the first place, how he knew where to build the altar. It was how he knew that I was going to be born. Did I ever tell you that story?

Sv: Yes, yes. Several times.

I: Oh… right. Well anyway, we pulled some stones together to build the altar. I had to do most of it because Dad's getting on a bit. Anyway, when we had finished, Dad tied me up and put me on the altar.

Sv: How?

I: What do you mean, how?

Sv: Well, how did he manage to lift you on to the altar?

I: There's no way he could have forced me to do it. He just told me he wanted to tie me up, and then he asked me to lie on the altar.

Sv: And you did it?

I: He did have the knife, but I didn't see how I could put up much of a fight. God had told him to do it, and if there is one thing I know about Dad, he absolutely trusts what God says. And what is the point of fighting against something that God wants?

Sv: But how did you know that

God had told him to do it?

I: Just think about the alternative. I know that Dad loves me, and I know he wouldn't want to kill me. And Dad always does what God tells him. And, God never seems to let him down. At the last minute, God told Dad to stop, and then showed him where to find a ram stuck in a bush. And we had our sacrifice. You should have seen the relief on his face.

Sv: I bet you were more than a bit relieved too, eh?

I: I'll say! I know Dad wasn't happy about it all, and I don't fully understand it, but there is one thing I do know.

Sv: What's that?

I: I have absolutely no doubt about Dad's faith and trust in God. I mean, he doesn't just talk about God or just offer him the odd sheep or goat from those huge flocks of his. He is prepared to do absolutely anything for God, and that's pretty impressive.

(Children under five may find the drama too complicated and graphic. As an alternative for them, you could take them into a huddle to read two stories from *The Big Bible Storybook* (SU) – 'A new place to live for Abraham' (page 26) and 'A new family for Abraham' (page 28). Talk about how much Abraham wanted a family and how his son Isaac was seen as a gift from God. Details of the book are on page 41.

After the drama (or reading), it will be important to draw attention to a number of the points highlighted by the characters. The primary point is that Abraham's faith was clearly much more than a theoretical or passive faith, but one of action and personal commitment. As a role model for Isaac, Abraham must have communicated a genuine trust in God like none other. Perhaps there is no better example of the advice that Jesus gave in Luke 14 explaining that people may be called to 'hate' their families in serving God/putting God first in everything.

The story also emphasises that:

- Abraham had already demonstrated his obedience a number of times – this was not a one-off event. God doesn't ask us just to be obedient once, but to follow wherever he leads.
- Abraham must have recognised the apparent conflict between the promise that he would be the father of a nation, and the call to sacrifice his only son. But Abraham still trusted that God knew what he was doing. Do we sometimes think that we know better than God and so disobey him?
- Given the ages of Abraham and Isaac, it is difficult to imagine Abraham getting him tied up on the altar without at least some co-operation. Perhaps Isaac displays here trust and obedience to his earthly father as a response to Abraham's trust and obedience to God. As tiny children we have to trust our parents. But when we're older, do we still trust that they want what's best for us or do we fight against them? As parents, how do we treat our children in such a way that we deserve their trust?
- It's important to *show* our commitment as well as *saying* we love God. How can we show others how much serving God means to us?
- If appropriate, invite one father to share some ideas on how he communicates the importance of his faith to his child(ren).

Prayers of confession

Explain that being a parent or mentor is probably the hardest job in the world! But God has given us the Holy Spirit to equip and guide us. But we still find it hard to do what's right, whether we're parents or children. Invite people to spend a brief time in silence confessing to God that we do not always do the right thing and that sometimes, through selfishness, we let God and others down.

Then ask everyone to stand up and hold out their hands as if to receive something. You will need to put the prayer on the next page on an acetate or PowerPoint. This is available as a download from **Fathers_2** www.scriptureunion.org.uk/light. Younger children can simply say the refrain, 'Please forgive us'.

Adults: Father God, we are sorry for the times when we have not set a good example to our children or those in our care. **Please forgive us.**

Children: Father God, we are sorry when we have not listened to those who set us a good example. **Please forgive us.**

All: Father God, we are sorry that we do not always put you first in our lives. **Please forgive us.**

All: Father God, may your Holy Spirit help us and guide us, to shape us into the people you want us to be. Amen.

Response

Abraham made it crystal clear to his son that his priority was to obey God and put him first. Using the card from the 'Thanksgiving' earlier, invite everyone to write or draw one way in which they can behave towards others (maybe, but not necessarily, the person already written on the card) that shows how committed they are to God. It may be something practical in caring for others, in the family, in the way we speak or in praying for others.

Prayers of intercession

Prior to the service, help some children and/or youth group members prepare prayers asking God to strengthen parents and carers as they bring up their children. If appropriate, pray especially for fathers. The following prayers are suggested:
Dear God, we thank you for our mums and dads who care for us every day, even when they are tired and may not feel like it. We pray that you will make them strong.
Dear God, our father in heaven, we thank you for the example of adults who know and love you and show us what it means to be a follower of Jesus. We pray that they will go on showing us the way to you.

Dear God, these are the things we really like about our dads _____. We pray for people who haven't got a dad or who rarely see him. Be especially close to them today.

Close by saying together The Lord's Prayer.

God's blessing

Close the service with the following words of blessing:

The grace of the Lord Jesus Christ
The love of our heavenly Father
And the fellowship of the Holy Spirit
Be with you all, and in all our relationships
Amen.

Elisha 5

JULY 2 Kings 4:1–7; John 2:1–12

Background

Today's Bible stories both illustrate God's great power and compassion, seen in small but miraculous ways that really mattered to the individuals concerned. They are far less dramatic than the miracle in 2 Kings 6 (see Outline on Elisha 4, February) when God protected the Israelites from their Syrian enemies and revealed the heavenly army. Instead, they are miracles that could be described as domestic ones, in response to the needs of two families who face the crisis of crippling debt or a social embarrassment. While the exact circumstances would not be found in the 21st century, everyone can identify with the emotion of both situations, including children and young people. (This is the last of the five outlines in the series on Elisha.)

The truth at the heart of both stories is that God identifies with our needs, whether big or small. Through them the congregation will be encouraged to have faith in a God who provides in unexpected ways and who requires us to actively put our trust in him. The two stories provide an interesting comparison with each other.

Today many people are doubtful and cynical about miracles, and even about the very existence of the God who performs them. While this is not a service to explore the validity and role of miracles in the Bible narrative, there may be those present, including outsiders, who will be prompted to think about miracles. But they will also be challenged by the ordinariness of these miracles, which may turn them in wonder and gratitude to the God who cares enough to meet people's needs. May this service help your congregation be re-enthused about God's compassion and the very real ways he performs miracles of provision even today. They will be reminded of the vital part everyone has to play in being used by God to provide for other people, and so become part of the miracle itself.

 **Link**

In July 2009, users of Scripture Union's *Light* curriculum material will have been looking at God's compassion as demonstrated by Jesus' care of others (including the story of Jesus changing water into wine) and in the picture of Jesus as the Good Shepherd – all from John's Gospel. God's compassion shown in the miracle performed by Elisha will effectively complement this theme.

Introduction

As people enter, give them a piece of paper and a pen/pencil. Ask everyone to draw three circles, one inside the other, on their paper, or provide a template to follow. Within the central circle, ask them to write the name of, or draw, the person who is closest to them. This could be their best friend, a parent, a relative or a husband/wife. In the second circle, write the name of, or draw, their five closest friends. In the outer circle, write the names of, or draw, some acquaintances. Around the edge of the paper, write the names of, or draw, areas in which they have influence, for example job, school, town, world. Younger children could do this in a larger group or with their family.

Now ask everyone to consider the needs of people within each of these groups – physical, social, emotional, spiritual or financial.

Underline the name of one person or sphere of social influence for whom they feel they might be able to provide some help, either as an individual, as a family, or as a church. If appropriate, ask for feedback, particularly about the ways in which the church can help fulfil the needs of groups and individuals. You will be returning to this in 'Response' towards the end of the service, when people will have had more time to think of the name they want to underline.

Alternatively, create a thought shower on a flip chart at the front of the room about the word 'Compassion'. (Younger children may not know this word so substitute it with 'Kindness' if they are likely to be present.) What does this word make people think of? Appoint a volunteer scribe to write down responses people call out. If you have access to a data projector, someone could type in people's answers as they call them out, to project onto a screen.

You could use this same idea to think about different needs which call out for an act of compassion. These could be categorised into personal needs, local needs, needs of the church and needs of the world. You will be returning to this towards the end of the service but if you have not done this activity, adapt what you say.

Praise

Sing together one or more of the following songs:

'Praise God from whom all blessings flow'
'O Lord my God in you I put my trust (Let the praises ring)'
'The Lord's my shepherd I'll not want'

Prayers of thanksgiving

In advance, ask a small group of people with acting skills to work out a series of ten things for which to thank God. Five are big things such as happiness, children, parents, a new job and five are to be small or everyday things such as a shower or breakfast this morning, a new dress, an email from a friend living a long way away, a sunny day, holidays. These ten things need to be presented in a way that makes it clear what they are, either by acting or miming or by using props. This is a variation on the game of charades.

As each thing is acted/mimed, invite everyone to guess what it is. Talk about the difference between big and small things. This might be debatable – an email from a friend may be an everyday occurrence or its content might be highly significant and life-changing. God cares about all our needs, whether they are big or small. Lead the congregation in thanksgiving with their eyes open:

We thank you, God, for… *(The small things are acted out.)*
We thank God because he provides for our small needs.
We thank you, God, for… *(The big things are acted out.)*
We thank God because he provides for our big needs.

Prayers of confession

You will need a flip chart, pen, (or OHP and acetate or data projector) and a volunteer to lead this time of confession. Ask your volunteer to write the word 'SORRY' vertically down the left side of the paper, starting with the letter 'S' in the top left corner, and ending with the letter 'Y' in the bottom left corner. Explain to the congregation that you are going to create an acrostic poem that also acts as a prayer of confession. It will be used to say sorry to God for the times we haven't identified with others' needs, for when we haven't asked him for the help we need, and when we have not trusted in God's amazing, abundant compassion.

To 'write' this poem, members of the congregation need to create five sentences, each one beginning with a different letter of the word 'sorry'. Ask your volunteer to write these sentences up in the correct order to create the poem. You may be spoilt for choice, in which case the leader will need to choose which contribution is the most suitable.

Your poem might go something like this:

Sorry for the times we forget you are the God of compassion
Open our eyes to see the needs of others
Repentance flows for those times we have messed up
Recognising our failures we come to you and admit we were wrong
You are good, and you forgive us. Thank you.

Once you have a completed poem, ask the congregation to read the poem together as a prayer.

This could be done in a small group or all together. Alternatively, two groups (a home group, Sunday children's/youth group or family) could create their own poem in advance and lead the congregation in two prayers of confession.

Reading the Bible

Before the service, ask two members of the congregation to prepare to read the following stories:

could use the story as we have it ✓

2 Kings 4:1–7
John 2:1–12

Both stories lend themselves to a dramatic reading. You could also read the version of the story about Elisha as it is retold in *The*

Strong Tower (SU) by Robert Harrison. This book makes the Bible story easily understood and is particularly relevant to children going through difficult times. Or you could watch an extract from *The Miracle Maker* of Jesus turning water into wine. Another video episode you could watch would be Episode 2 of the *Wastewatchers* DVD (SU). Both of these would bring this miraculous event to life for the congregation.

Bible talk

Don't need to use volunteers?

Before the service you will need to prepare five large (A3) pieces of card. On one side of each card, draw a large question mark. On the other side write one of the following questions on each:

1. Who is in need?
2. What is the need?
3. Who can help?
4. How can they help?
5. Why should they help?

Before the service begins, hide these pieces of card around the room. Ask five (or more) volunteers to go in search of them. Having found a card, a volunteer comes to the front to hold up their card with just the question mark on show. Explain that you want them to answer the questions on the back of these cards, in relation to the stories they have just heard. (Answer each question about the Elisha story first so that the likelihood of younger children getting confused between the two stories is reduced.)

Ask the volunteer who is holding the card with the first question ('Who is in need?') to turn their card around and read out their question. Make the point that in both Bible stories, there are characters who are in serious need. Ask the congregation to identify who these characters are. Then ask them to think about the needs in this world. Think back to the earlier discussion where everyone might have considered the needs of those they know, from their closest friends to their acquaintances. Remind them

that there are people in need everywhere we look.

Get the volunteer with the second question ('What is the need?') to turn their card around and read out the question. Ask people to say what the needs are in each of the Bible stories. You will need to fill in some background. Oil was an essential commodity for cooking, lighting and for medicinal purposes. It was therefore valuable enough to pay off a debt. The embarrassment of the host at the wedding in Cana cannot be underestimated. Guests needed to be well provided for and a grave mistake had been made. The amount of high quality wine that Jesus makes available would have been staggering.

Make the point that it was necessary to identify what the problem was in order to be able to fix it. Again, you could refer back to the earlier discussion. Needs come in all shapes and sizes, but as we see from both of these stories, God cares about them.

Ask the third volunteer to turn round their card and read out their question. ('Who can help?') Make the point that in both stories, after a need has been identified, someone is there who might be able to help. The widow goes to Elisha who is a respected prophet, probably from the same group of prophets as her late husband. It is Jesus' mother who identifies the need for more wine at the wedding in Cana, and she goes to Jesus for help. Challenge the congregation to think about who they go to in a time of need. Do they ask God for help? Who do they trust to help them? Ask them to think about how much faith they have that God cares for them and will provide if they go to him.

Ask the fourth volunteer to read out the question on their card. ('How can they help?') Elisha helped the widow by performing a miracle in which her small amount of oil was multiplied. She was then able to sell it, pay off her late husband's debts and live off the profits. (This is an interesting example of enabling someone to take responsibility for getting themselves out of trouble.) Jesus turned water into huge quantities of wine of the very best quality.

When we go to God in prayer he has compassion on us and acts. Point out that in both of these stories God provides in a very practical way. Both the widow and the servants are required to do something that doesn't

make a lot of sense. They are required to trust and obey before God helps them out. Their faith is tested and put into action. What might God be asking us to do? Are we listening? If you personally have a story of how God has asked you to do something that seemed ridiculous at the time in answer to prayer, you might like to share it.

Ask the fifth volunteer to read out the question on their card. ('Why should they help?') God's compassion and power are evident in both these stories. In what ways can we be used by God to provide for other people? The generosity of the neighbours in giving their jars to the widow was used by God to provide for the needs of someone they knew. Refer back to the associations you may have made with the word 'Compassion' or 'Kindness'. Which qualities do we need to focus on developing, in order to be more available for God to use?

Prayers of intercession

If the church is already committed to a project of compassion, use this involvement as the focus of prayer. If this is not possible, choose one area of contemporary need and ask God to demonstrate his powerful compassion. In advance, work with a group of children or young people to write out prayers structured around the five questions in the previous talk.

We know that _____ is in need of _____
We know that you are a God of compassion and you want to help them but you may need us to play our part.
We ask that you will make us ready to help by
_____
We pray that _____
We want to be involved because we love you, the God of compassion.
Amen.

Show on screen

Use flashup project we sent word to

time for people to pray

again in silence

people or situation they unitially came up with

Finish with response on next page

Response

Ask the congregation to discuss with the people near them any practical ideas of how they can help to provide for the needs of others, especially anyone they have thought about in the course of the service. This could be personal action or action by the church family or the wider church.

Then say together the following promise:

Lord God, you are full of compassion.
We commit ourselves this week to look out for the needs of others, to help them in prayer and action.

May others see that you are a God of compassion and kindness through the way we act.

Sing one or more of these songs as a response and sign of commitment to recognise the God of compassion in our attitudes, prayers and actions toward others:

'Don't let my love grow cold (Light the fire again)'
'Oh kneel me down again (God of the broken)'
'We bow down and confess (You are all I need)'

God's blessing

Read out the following prayer for the people of the congregation:

The Lord bless you and protect you.
The Lord show you mercy and kindness.
The Lord be good to you and give you peace.

Matthew 1

AUGUST Proverbs 16:9; 19:21; Matthew 9:9–12

Background

God has had a divine plan for the salvation of humankind from the beginning of time. He chose to involve people in making this plan a reality, people who were often scared, weak, vulnerable, sinful and rebellious. The people God used had their moments of greatness – Moses parting the Red Sea, Abraham being prepared to sacrifice Isaac, Peter walking on water, but equally they had their moments of shame and failure – Moses' disobedience with the water and the rock, Abraham lying about his wife to Pharaoh. Jesus' death and resurrection, of course, were the climax of God's plan of salvation.

In this service we will explore how Jesus called people to follow him, to be part of his plan. In particular we will take a look at Jesus calling Matthew, in Matthew 9:9–12. On first reading about this, it can seem very much as if Jesus just happened to be walking along, saw Matthew and thought, 'Ah yes, good choice, I'll have him'. Yet as Luke 6:12–16 indicates, Jesus spent a whole night in prayer before making public his choice of disciples. His encounter with Matthew was not accidental. It was part of his plan.

The choice of Matthew, a tax collector, is an unlikely one. Tax collectors were seen as collaborators with the Roman authorities, were disliked by many and thought of as dishonest. Jesus' team of disciples were an altogether unlikely band. But he didn't choose the 'righteous', the obvious candidates, but the 'sinners'. That is as true now as it was then. He doesn't choose the wise things but the foolish. He values all people and leads them into unexpected roles. As you explore this theme together, be prepared to discover more of the plan that God has for you as a church and as individuals.

 **Link**

During August 2009, users of Scripture Union's *Light* curriculum material will be exploring God's plan as it was worked out in the life of Joseph (Genesis 37–45). The call of Matthew provides a New Testament balance. During August you may run a series of all-age services instead of your regular Sunday groups. This volume provides two series of services – five on Elisha and three from Matthew's Gospel. This is the first in the Matthew series.

Introduction

Introduce the theme of God's plan for his people by acknowledging some of those involved in the plan as it unfolds throughout the Bible. Set up a quick quiz about people God used. Extra points can be awarded to anyone who can say what might be seen as areas of strength or weakness in these characters. (There may be more than one answer!) You could split the congregation into two teams or alternatively ask two families to compete with each other. However you choose to do it, keep the quiz moving quickly. (Some of the clues will be easier for children, so ask them first.) The clues, answers and likely areas of strength and weakness (there are others) are as follows:

Clues	Answers	Weakness	Strength
Dream boy with big ideas	Joseph	Proud	Persistent
Shepherd boy who wrote songs	David	Commits adultery	Loved God
Father of all God's people	Abraham	Lies about Sarah being his wife	Faithful
Abraham's wife	Sarah	Laughs at news of having a child	Protective mother
Takes his brother's birthright	Jacob	Deceives brother	Wrestled with God
Swallowed by big fish	Jonah	Runs away from God	Obeyed God
Asks God for wisdom	Solomon	Loves foreign wives	Wise
Man with supernatural strength	Samson	Gives away secret of strength	Judge
Puts out a woollen fleece	Gideon	Fearful	Judge
Walks on water (briefly!)	Peter	Denies Jesus	Brave
One of 12 in charge of money	Judas	Betrays Jesus	Respected treasurer
Asks to see Jesus' hands and side	Thomas	Doubts Jesus	Saw Jesus as God

Sometimes God uses the most unlikely characters to bring about his plans. Just like us, these characters have flaws and areas of weakness. Explain that you are going to look at yet another unlikely character whom Jesus called to follow him.

Praise

Using an OHT projector or PowerPoint put the following words on the screen, taken from Psalm 33:1–3. Say the words in regular type and ask the congregation to shout out the words in bold, as a response:

Sing joyfully to the Lord, you righteous;
It is fitting for the upright to praise him.
Praise the Lord with the harp
Make music to him on the ten-stringed lyre.
Sing to him a new song;
Play skilfully, and shout for joy.

(This is available as a download from **Matthew 1** www.scriptureunion.org.uk/light)

Then sing one or more of the following songs:

'Praise him you heavens and all that's above'
'Give thanks to the Lord, our God and King'
'Great is your faithfulness' (Chris Tomlin)

Reading the Bible

Either read yourself, or ask a volunteer or volunteers, prepared in advance, to read the following passages from the Bible:

**Proverbs 16:9 and Proverbs 19:21
Matthew 9:9–12**

Prayers of thanksgiving

Prepare in advance enough paper footprint shapes, one for each person. Use smaller ones for children and larger ones for adults. Give these out as people come in to the service. Also have a wall or board available, so that you can stick the footprints onto it, and a supply of Blu-tack.

Introduce this by saying how we can look back on our lives and see that Proverbs 16:9 is true: we can make plans but we can see that God is ultimately in control of our lives and guides our steps. Ask each person to think of a time when they have known God has guided them or called them to do something or been especially close to them. Younger children could be helped to think of a time at school or when they have felt sad or ill. The footprint is a symbol of this time. As everyone holds their footprint, thank God that he is with us and does guide us.

Then encourage everyone to stick their 'footprint' to the wall or on the board, at random, in thankfulness to God. You could have some reflective music playing in the background.

When everyone has finished, point out that although our footprints seem to be going in many different directions, God knows the next step for each of our lives and he will guide us.

Bible talk

The Bible teaching in this service requires the performance of a monologue – 'Follow me'. You will need a confident reader to practise this in advance. Ideally, the performer should learn the script by heart. It could be performed sitting or standing and a microphone needs to be used. He or she could be dressed in the costume of a tax collector.

Begin by saying that we don't really know much about Matthew apart from the fact that he was a tax collector who is attributed with writing Matthew's Gospel. He was also known as Levi. The word 'tax collector' suggests he was a 'customs official', probably stationed at a booth located at or near Capernaum and the Sea of Galilee and the major trade route between Asia and Europe. The tax booth would have stood high above the ground, like a lifeguard station on a beach. It was designed to help see what was happening all around. This meant that a tax collector would quickly spot any traders who crossed the border into Galilee and would come down to collect the taxes due on their goods. He would have collected taxes on all goods that crossed the border into Galilee. A specified percentage would be paid to the Roman authorities and then the tax collector was free to determine the rest travellers had to pay in order for him to make a profit. No wonder tax collectors were regarded as dishonest and were disliked.

Ask the congregation to imagine what it might have been like to be Matthew. Would they have minded being disliked, or would having lots of money be sufficient compensation? Say that today they have an opportunity to hear from Matthew himself. Perhaps the day he met Jesus went something like this…

(This is the cue for your performer to start reading the script.)

'Follow me' monologue script

It seemed like any other working day to me. The sun was already hot as I walked the well-worn road to the tax booth, down by the harbour. As usual, people glared at me, ignored me or even spat in disgust. I'm a tax collector, you see – well, I prefer to call myself a customs official – and we're not well-liked. It's not surprising I suppose, seeing as we demand money from people who are just trying to make a living out of trading their goods. Added to that, we give a percentage to the Roman government and keep the rest for ourselves. A lot of people think we're being dishonest – I just see it as earning good money. It was the money that attracted me to the job, that and meeting people from lots of different countries. I love watching the traders coming and going. But sometimes I wonder if there's more to life than this. The evil looks I get wear me down.

On this particular morning, as I turned the corner that leads to the booth, I noticed something unusual. A group of children was gathered around talking excitedly together. I caught some of what they were saying before they met my eye and scurried off. They've been taught to hate people like me too.
'Did you see? He picked up his mat and walked! Just like that!' said one boy.
'Well, did you hear the one about the pigs?' a little girl retorted.

It's been like this for several days now. Snippets of conversation, more and more about Jesus, the great healer and miracle maker. There is a sense of expectancy in the air… something inside me was beginning to stir. But I quickly turned my thoughts to other matters. I have a job to do. I climbed the steps to the top of the booth where I get a clear view of the boats in the harbour and any passing traders who need to pay me their taxes. Once I spot someone, quick as a flash, I'm out there collecting their money. But that day it was quiet, so I spent the first few hours catching up on paperwork.

At about 11 o'clock, I glanced up and saw a large crowd of people heading towards my booth. My goodness, had they gone mad? Normally, people steer well clear of me! Then I realised they were following a man and he was looking directly at me. For some reason I felt slightly uncomfortable by his gaze and I looked away. But I knew his eyes were fixed on me and I had to look at him. I was shocked to notice something in his eyes I haven't seen for months, years even. Something long forgotten – a look of complete acceptance and love. For me? Wow, for me! He spoke. His voice was gentle but had authority. He only said two words: 'Follow me'.

At that instant I knew this was the moment I'd been waiting for, searching for, yes longing for. And I didn't waste a second. I got up and followed him. Just like that! Looking back now it seems strange that I was that decisive, but I was desperate and I knew this man was someone special. I was so excited I decided to hold a big party the next evening – wine, food, music, dancing. I invited lots of my tax collector friends and others who weren't seen as particularly 'good folk'. (Most of us were banned from worshipping in the temple.) But Jesus came and he brought his friends with him. Suddenly, a silence fell on the party. The Pharisees had arrived. They always put a dampener on everything. Immediately the atmosphere changed and we started to feel uncomfortable.

'Why do you eat with tax collectors and sinners?' they asked Jesus in an accusing tone of voice. Good question. Why *did* he want to spend time with us?

Jesus' reply took some thinking about. I think he did that deliberately to outwit them! He said that it was sick people who need a doctor, not healthy people. Equally, he hadn't come to call the 'righteous' but 'sinners'.

I looked into the eyes of one of the Pharisees. I knew what he was thinking: I keep all the Law of Moses; I am a righteous man. Somehow, I knew this wasn't true. Not for him, not for me, not for any of us. I was a sinner, but so was he. It was then I realised Jesus knew a lot more about me than I'd first thought. I suspect that it wasn't just by chance that he passed my booth that day but that he'd planned it a long time ago. I wonder what other unexpected things he has in store for me.

After the delivery of the monologue, initiate a discussion with the congregation on how far they think Jesus had planned to call Matthew to follow him that day. Talk about whether they think Matthew would have regretted his decision to follow Jesus. Ask what things he might have missed about his old way of life and what things he would have enjoyed instead. Encourage the congregation to participate as much as possible by moving around the room and using a roving mike for people to speak into. Remember to include contributions from children and young people.

Conclude by asking the congregation to reflect on what it would be like if Jesus turned up in person today at their place of work/school/college. How might they respond? What difference does Jesus make? Ask if anyone misses their old way of life. What do they enjoy instead? You might need to prepare some responses from people in advance.

Prayers of confession

Ask the congregation to think back to those people in the Bible we looked at earlier in the quiz, people who had strengths and weaknesses. We are no different from them. We have strengths and weakness and we also fail to do what God calls us to do. Invite everyone to join you in this prayer of confession where the congregational responses are in bold type:

Father God, sometimes we have been like Joseph, proud of our own achievements rather than depending on you.
We're sorry. Please forgive us.
Sometimes we've been like Gideon, fearful of standing up for you and telling others about you.
We're sorry. Please forgive us.
Sometimes we've been like Sarah and laughed at the plans you have for us because we've lacked faith to believe they will happen.
We're sorry. Please forgive us.
Sometimes, Lord, we've been like Jonah and have tried to run away from you because we're not sure we're up to the task.
We're sorry. Please forgive us.
Lord, thank you that just as you used these people from the Bible, despite their weaknesses and failings, you can use us to make your plans happen. Amen.

Prayers of intercession

People are always having to make choices – which school to go to, who to be friends with, whether to change job, move house, take on a new responsibility in church, to give up a role in the community, how to vote in an election. How do we make decisions? How does God guide us?

Ask everyone to think of one decision they have to make in the next few weeks. After a few moments invite everyone to stand and hold out their hands, palms upwards. Then turn their arms outwards from the elbow as though they have two options.

Lord God, we often have two choices to make. We can choose to do one thing or we can do another. Please help us to know what is the best decision.
(If you know of choices people have to make that are public knowledge, or that the church as a whole has to make, pray specifically about these.)
Lord God, we are part of your plan. Help us willingly to follow you and do what's right, whatever our strengths or weaknesses. Amen.

Response

Everyone plays a short game of 'Simon Says'. Then explain that following Jesus isn't always as simple as that. Some of us may have lost our way, or have failed to respond to God's call in the past. Some of us may have never said 'yes' to following God. Make time for people to respond here as necessary. One of the songs could be played quietly in the background. Encourage people to think about how they want to follow God afresh. See below for details of booklets to help you in this.

Then sing one or more of these worship songs as a way of responding to God:

'I will offer up my life'
'Beautiful Lord, wonderful Saviour'
'Before the world began, you were on his mind'
'Will you come and follow me?'
'I want to serve the purpose of God'

God's blessing

For an original blessing why not get a few young people to perform the following as a rap. Give them plenty of notice so they have time to practise it. The syllables to emphasise are shown in bold:

Hey **you**, **broth**er have you **got** what it **takes**
To **follow** God com**pletely** what**ever** the **stakes**?
Did you **know**, **sister**, God is **call**ing **you**
To **trust** God **fully** with the **plans** he has for **you**?
God's **love** is **great**, there's **no one** he'll **exclude**,
So **receive** God's **blessing** all you **super**-cool **dudes**!

Following Jesus booklets

Friends with Jesus
(for 5 to 7s)

These booklets will help you explain to children and young people what it means to follow Jesus, forever. Sold as single copies or in packs of 20 they are available from good local Christian bookshops or from SU Mail Order.

Me and Jesus (for 8 to 10s)

Jesus=friendship forever
(for 10 to 12s)

For more details visit www.scriptureunion.org.uk.

Matthew 2

AUGUST Matthew 9:18–26; Genesis 50:15–21

Background

The story in Matthew 9:18–26 features two miracles that are also found in Mark 5:21–43 and Luke 8:40–56. Matthew's account is shorter than the other Gospels, as he often does with descriptions of miracles. There are two main characters who approach Jesus.

The versions in the other Gospels add additional information to the account in Matthew. For example, the 'ruler' is actually the ruler of the synagogue, called Jairus. As such he was responsible for the order and progress of worship in the synagogue, a local meeting place for observers of Judaism. Although Jairus approaches Jesus, he does so on behalf of his 12-year-old daughter. She is as good as dead and when Jesus finally gets to the house the mourners are already there earning their fee by leading the community in emotional wailing. Everyone, except Jesus, assumes that she is a hopeless case.

The second person to come to Jesus is a woman who has been bleeding for 12 years. This bleeding doesn't appear to put her in immediate physical danger but, perhaps more importantly, it has left her in a state of uncleanliness (see Leviticus 15:19–33) and unable to play a full role in society. She is an outsider and an outcast.

Jesus takes control of the situation and performs the miracles. Both the woman and the young girl have their lives transformed by him. The woman, who has been unclean, can now re-enter society with a renewed faith in God. But there were others involved in the story who could have had their lives transformed too. Jairus, and maybe those in his family, showed great faith; the crowd as witnesses saw two people exercising their faith; and the mourners went from crying, to mocking, to gossiping the news. As for the young girl, she was fairly passive throughout!

An encounter with Jesus can transform life. That is the challenge of this service.

 **Link**

During August 2009, users of Scripture Union's *Light* curriculum material will be exploring God's plan as it was worked out in the life of Joseph (Genesis 37–45). It must have been difficult for Jairus, as his daughter lay dying, to believe that God had a good purpose for his life. Joseph must have wondered that too as he languished in jail. During August you may run a series of all-age services instead of your regular Sunday groups. This volume provides two series of services – five on Elisha and three from Matthew's Gospel. This is the second in the Matthew series.

Introduction

Before the service, browse the Internet to find images of the latest rock and pop celebrities. Show these images on an OHT or projector as a visual focus. Invite two of the young people to guess who the images are. If you don't have pictures, invite the young people to name one or two of their favourite celebrities. Extend this to older members of the congregation. Once you have a few names, ask how you could get close to these people and learn more about them (buy their music, visit their website, wear badges, hang posters, see them in concert). If any of these answers aren't forthcoming, feed them into the discussion.

Explain that seeing them in concert is probably the closest many of us will get to a celebrity. However, you could hang around outside and perhaps get their autograph as they leave. Ultimately, getting to meet someone would be the best encounter possible. Ask if anyone in the congregation has met their favourite singers and how it happened. Comment that quite often crowds surround a celebrity when they are out. In today's service you'll be meeting some people who met Jesus in a big crowd. Their lives were changed by the encounter.

Reading the Bible

Either read the following two Bible passages yourself, or ask two members of the congregation in advance to come prepared to read them.

Matthew 9:18–26
Genesis 50:15–21

The Genesis reading makes the link with the story of Joseph that has been explored in *Light*. If you are using the monologue you may prefer to only read Genesis 50.

Bible talk

The main part of the Bible teaching is covered in four monologues which you can in a variety of ways. You could perform each of them yourself, changing one piece of clothing, probably some headgear, to differentiate between the people. Alternatively four different people could present the monologues. It will need to be planned and practised beforehand.

Another way of presenting this, which would be really very powerful, is to record the monologues onto video and play them back via projectors onto a screen. There is some extra text provided in order to present the monologues as 'interviews' in a news report. If you don't use the monologues in this way, simply replace the text with a short introduction.

Jairus' monologue:
(**Interviewer:** Thank you for agreeing to be interviewed, Mr Jairus. Could you tell us, in your own words, what happened today?)
Jairus: My daughter hadn't been well, not well at all, in fact my wife and I had been increasingly worried about her. She seemed to be slowly drifting away. We didn't know what was wrong but she was getting worse and worse, thinner and thinner. We asked the local health service (nothing like as good as you have today) if they knew what was wrong. They didn't, and they told us to prepare for the worst. My wife and I were desperate. Then she mentioned the name 'Jesus'. We knew that this man had been performing miracles and healing people in the local area so, as a last resort, I decided to go to ask Jesus for help. There had been a lot of discussion about him in the synagogue where I'm the leader. Is he someone who loves being a celebrity? Is he a magician? Has he come from God? I believed that if he really was sent from God, he would be able to help. So off I went to ask Jesus to help my daughter get better. The rest is history.

Woman's monologue:

(**Interviewer:** Let's now turn to the woman who interrupted Jesus on his way to Jairus' house. Thank you for coming to speak to us. Could you explain what happened, in your own words?)

Woman: I'm just so happy. I can't stop smiling. (*Giggles.*) My illness was very personal. It kept me from doing everyday things that other people take for granted. I wasn't even allowed to get involved in worshipping God. And people didn't like me. They said I was smelly. But I heard rumours about the sort of things Jesus has done and said. I believed he was sent by God and I knew, deep down, that he could help me. But it took me a long time to get to where he was and when I got there the crowd was huge. I pushed my way through to get to the front, and that annoyed a lot of people. As I got closer, I realised I would have to act quickly and that all I had to do was touch his cloak. If I could do that, I would be better. I got there. I reached out and… sorry, I'm just too happy, I can't explain what happened but I felt a power flow through my body. I was better. Just like that. My life has been transformed.

Crowd member's monologue:

(**Interviewer:** We've heard from the woman who pushed through the crowd. Let's hear from someone in that crowd. Can you tell us what happened?)

Crowd member: Oh, what happened, yea, well, I was walking along with my friends and got caught in this moving crowd with the miracle man, Jesus, in the middle. He's the big thing at the moment, the top celeb in Capernaum's, well A-list. It's all because a lot of amazing things are happening around him. The leader from the synagogue had just spoken to Jesus. (He's important so he got to Jesus easily.) He asked Jesus to help his daughter. I can't remember whether he said she was dead or almost dead. Either way, when Jesus agreed to go with him a buzz went around the crowd. Something was going to happen. Just then someone stuck their elbow in me, trying to get to Jesus. It was one of the weird people who hang around town, one of the outcasts. We don't like people like that. But this woman, she just pushed her way to Jesus and grabbed hold of his cloak, just for a second. Jesus stopped at once and spoke to her. I could see the synagogue guy getting restless and jumpy but Jesus stopped for this woman. No one cares about this woman, but Jesus did.

Professional mourner's monologue:

(**Interviewer:** This woman seems to have slowed down Jesus' journey to Jairus' house. When he got there at last, there were already mourners. You can guess what had happened while Jairus was away. We'll talk to one of these mourners.)

Mourner: I still can't believe what happened. I'd been hired, along with my flute-playing work colleagues, to attend the official mourning of Jairus' daughter. She'd just died, despite her father's efforts to get hold of Jesus, a local healer. There we were, playing and crying out loud when along comes Jesus. He'd got a big crowd with him too, talking about some woman who had already been healed. We told Jesus not to bother. The girl was dead and we were sending her off with the highest quality wails that money can buy. And do you know what Jesus said? He told us to go away and that the girl was only sleeping. We had a good old laugh at that. But we were pushed out and, after spending some time in the house, Jesus came out with the girl. She's alive, up and raring to go. I can't believe it and I was there.

Once the monologues have been played or acted out, ask the congregation to think about which of the characters in the story is most like them. There's the woman and Jairus, who both needed Jesus to do something to help and they trusted him. There are the people in the crowd who didn't do anything to help the woman, in fact, they made it hard for her. They disliked her. There are also the mourners, just doing their job without thinking about what was really going on. Finally there is the little girl who didn't understand much, but her life was dramatically transformed!

Write up the following phrases, each on a large card, beside the symbol:

Needed something badly and trusted Jesus

Opposed what was going on and did not help

Just did their job and not interested

Just not aware of what is going on

Display these symbols and phrases as you explain how each is linked to one or more people in the story. Which of these, if any, do people identify with? Who are they in the story? This raises the question of how much do we trust Jesus? The fact remains that Jesus can transform lives.

Some people know how much they need Jesus to do for them and be with them. They trust him, even though they may not know much about him (Jairus and the woman).

Some people try to stop other people from coming to Jesus. They judge others and exclude them (the crowd).

Some people are just not interested and are busy with the demands of life (the mourners).

Some people for a variety of reasons are not aware of what is going on (the little girl).

Praise

Use any of the following songs, either in a specific time of musical worship or during the service. Each one could be introduced as a song praising God for the way he loves us:

'Thank you Jesus'
'Tell out my soul'
'Hosanna, Hosanna'
'Give thanks to the Lord, our God and King'
'Thank you for saving me'

Prayers of intercession

This can be done in several ways. The idea is to create a 'cloak' at the front of the church on which the congregation can write or draw their prayers and then 'touch'/attach them to the cloak, as the woman did. You will need a large piece of material or a coat/cloak that can be placed at the front, Post-it notes and pens/pencils.

A more visually striking suggestion is to nail two pieces of wood together to create a cross. On this cross hang either a long coat or a cloak (a hat stand would also work). Each person writes or draws their prayer and, with pins, attaches the prayers to the cloak. As a safety precaution, young children will need helpers to do this.

Explain that, like the woman in the story, we can approach Jesus, whatever barriers or obstacles we may encounter. In faith we can talk to him. Spend a few moments of quiet, then each person writes their prayer on the paper. It could be a request, an item of praise, a confession or even an outpouring of love to God. Once the prayer has been written, ask the congregation to bring their prayers to the front and attach them to the cloak, in faith and with no barriers.

Explain that after the services the prayers will be thrown away so no one will see what is written.

Response

Explain that the mourners were often professional and paid to come along and 'cry' with the family. Ask people to make a sad, wailing noise, then ask everyone to laugh and cheer and make any other happy sounds. After a few moments ask for quiet.

Explain that you are going to respond to the message of this story that Jesus can transform people's lives. The response will be from a state of sadness (shown by making quiet, wailing sounds) to one of joy (shown by clapping and cheers). The sign for sadness is your hands cupped upside down in a sad mouth shape. The sign for happiness is your hands cupped upwards. When the sign is made, everyone makes the appropriate sound. Emphasise that this is a serious time, not a time for silliness!

God who knows when we are miserable and afraid,

You know when we don't trust you.

You know when we stop other people from trusting you.

God who knows when we are joyful and glad,

You are happy when we trust you to change us or change a difficult situation.

You delight when we are glad.

Help us to expect you to transform and change our lives. Amen.

If it is the custom in your church, now would be a natural time to share the peace.

Prayers of confession

Jesus was surrounded by a crowd because of the many wonderful things he was doing. People wanted to see him and find out more. However, the two people who approached Jesus came in different ways. Jairus, being a respected, religious leader, a celebrity, found it easy to reach Jesus. The woman, on the other hand, was an outcast, whom nobody wanted to be seen with, let alone allow to be seen by Jesus. It was a lot more difficult for her to reach Jesus. Ask the congregation to join you in this prayer of confession, for the times when we don't treat people in the right way.

You could put this on an OHT or projector for everyone to join in:

Dear Lord, you showed compassion to the outsider.
You showed love to the woman who was not loved.
You changed the life of someone nobody wanted to change.
Forgive us for the times we have failed to love those whom others don't like.
Fill us with your Spirit and transform our lives,
So we can lead others to you.
Amen.

Prayers of thanksgiving

For the last songs of the service, ask all the children to come to the front to play musical instruments, celebrating the great things Jesus has done and can do. Have a selection of percussion instruments for them to bang, clang and hit. You may need to make some with empty containers and dried pulses. Choose songs of thanksgiving that are well known, with a strong beat.

God's blessing

Father God, we ask that you will bless each one of us as we leave this place of worship. We ask that you will be with us as we walk with the crowds.

We ask that you will shine in our lives, transforming us to bring others to you. Amen.

Bible stories

Reading Bible stories to an all-age congregation is a great way of bringing the Bible alive. These two books have been written to be used in the family, a small group or a larger congregation.

£7.99

£12.99

The Strong Tower

Ten retold Bible stories about children who found themselves in tough times.

The Big Bible Storybook

188 Bible stories to enjoy together. Meet the much-loved 'Bible friends' characters on every page.

For more details visit www.scriptureunion.org.uk.

Harvest/Matthew 3

SEPTEMBER Psalm 136:1–9, 23–26; Matthew 6:25–34

Background

Celebration of God's care for us has always been central in the life of God's people. The Israelites came together each year for the Festival of Tabernacles (Leviticus 23:33–43; Deuteronomy 16:13–17) to celebrate all God had given them – and as a reminder of how he had cared for them on their journey from Egypt to the Promised Land. This was a time of joyful re-affirmation of their trust in him. At the heart of this celebration was also a call to demonstrate God's generosity and his welcome to others (Deuteronomy 16:14). This festival, which Jesus and his disciples also celebrated (John 7:1–13), expressed their dependence on God.

Christians draw on this teaching in the Bible when they come together to celebrate their harvest festival. Whilst it's a time to give thanks to God and rejoice in all he has provided, it inevitably raises questions about those who have little – especially in places of famine and poverty. But, of course, the Israelites themselves went through times of hardship and famine as well as times of plenty. Centuries later, Paul talks about being content whatever his situation, because he trusted in God (Philippians 4:10–13). So, a harvest festival is an occasion to be challenged about how much we depend on God whatever our own circumstances, and about how we demonstrate his care to others in need.

At a previous service, ask the congregation to bring to this service harvest gifts, food to share and financial gifts as appropriate – see pages 91 and 95. You'll need a team of helpers to help with the harvest meal (or other refreshments) that follows and to distribute harvest gifts. Make your meeting area a special place with harvest decoration which will help create a sense of anticipation as the congregation arrives. Prepare enough copies of the cut-out hands for every person and give these to people as they arrive. The PowerPoint slide show and the hands image for cutting out can be downloaded from www.scriptureunion.org.uk/light.

If you are using this outline as just the third in the series on Matthew, you may want to downplay the emphasis on harvest. However, harvest themes are relevant throughout the year.

 **Link**

During September 2009, users of Scripture Union's *Light* curriculum material are looking at how God challenges us, based on how Jesus called people to respond to his challenge in Luke's Gospel. This outline complements this theme.

Introduction

As people arrive, aim to give them an immediate sense of God's care and provision in creation and hence the challenge to trust him. Prepare your service area to look as abundant and fruitful as possible, with flowers, greenery, fruit, vegetables, wheat, natural materials, as resources allow. At the front, begin a display of foodstuffs on tables to which the congregation will later add.

As people arrive, give them a copy of the hands cut-out. Have a PowerPoint slide show running (you'll find a ready-prepared one on the *All-Age Service Annual Vol 2* website at **Harv/Matt 3_1** www.scriptureunion.org.uk/light) to suggest God's lavish provision. Images might include: foods; fruit and vegetables growing or being harvested; people eating together; food advertisements; water; rainforests; birds; barns; flowers; clothes (Matthew 6:25–34). Include images from different parts of the world (eg tea being harvested). Include one or two images showing people suffering in places where there is famine. On a few of the slides include verses from the Bible readings to remind people that God cares and provides for his creation; the challenge is to trust him, freeing us to live for him. (If you don't have PowerPoint facilities use OHP acetates instead to display suitable images.)

Play background music to encourage praise and thanksgiving. This could include some of the suggestions from the 'Praise' section. Depending on your congregation and musicians, people could join in with songs of praise which they know.

In welcoming everyone explain that you have come together to celebrate God's care and provision and to be challenged afresh to live for him, trusting him for all your needs.

What's my name? (optional extra activity) This is a light-hearted general knowledge quiz which people could do as they arrive and then later during the harvest lunch at the end of the service. It draws on the ideas from the creation account in Genesis 1,2 where God creates all kinds of fruit-bearing trees, animals, etc, and gives Adam the task of naming the animals.

Before the service, display around your meeting area 20 pictures of different fruits, vegetables, butterflies, animals and birds. Include ones that people of all ages are likely to know and one or two more obscure ones (eg star fruit, red kite). Number each picture. Give each person a pencil and piece of paper which has a left-hand column numbered 1–20. The goal is to see who can name each part of God's creation in the 20 pictures. Give out the answers during the harvest lunch.

Prayers of thanksgiving

If you have notified people in advance, they will have come prepared for a harvest service, bringing gifts such as fresh fruit and vegetables, tins, packets, garden flowers. Have some extras available for any child who hasn't brought anything so that they can be involved in the following.

Explain that this service is an opportunity to thank God for *all* his care for us (not just food), such as having enough to eat, clothes, homes, education, hospitals and doctors, families, church, safety. In a brief time of quiet, invite people to focus on the harvest gift they have brought, prompting them to reflect on God's care for them and their families. People could also think of those who have been involved in the production of these items, such as farmers, workers in faraway countries, supermarket staff. Encourage everyone to turn their thoughts into prayers of thanksgiving.

Express your thanks to God aloud as you join together in the following responsive reading of verses from Psalm 136 (verses 1–9; 23–26). If possible display the response via a data projector or OHP. Someone with a strong voice reads the first part of each verse confidently and joyfully, in a way which invites the whole congregation to join in with the response, as follows:

Verse 1
Give thanks to the Lord, for he is good.
His love endures for ever.
Etc.

After verse 9, invite everyone to stand together and to speak or shout the response as though they really want to thank God. Continue at verse 23, reading to the end of the psalm, for example, as follows:
Verse 23
He remembered us in our low estate
His love endures for ever.
As people are standing, invite them now to come to the front and lay their harvest gifts on the table, joining the other things already placed there. As people are doing this, encourage them to keep thanking God. During this time, the musicians could quietly play some of the songs from the 'Praise' section below.

Praise

The following hymns and songs could be used in a time of praise and at other times indicated in the service:

'Praise God from whom all blessings flow'
'Now thank we all our God'

'Give thanks with a grateful heart'
'Come on and celebrate'
'I will enter his gates with thanksgiving in my heart'
'Come, ye thankful people, come'
'Seek ye first the kingdom of God'

Reading the Bible

Ask two volunteers to prepare a reading of **Matthew 6:25–34**, taking turns to read the different sections. For example:

Reader 1: verse 25
Reader 2: verses 26,27
Reader 1: verses 28,29
Reader 2: verse 30

Verse 31
Reader 1: So do not worry, saying,
Reader 2: What shall we eat?
Reader 1: or…
Reader 2: What shall we drink?
Reader 1: or…
Reader 2: What shall we wear?

Reader 1: verses 32,33
Reader 2: verse 34

Old Testament reading: **Psalm 136:1–9; 23–26** (see 'Prayers of Thanksgiving').

Bible talk

Display via data projector (or OHP) the image of hands outstretched towards the congregation (find an example on the *All-Age Service Annual Vol 2* website at **Harv/Matt 3_2** www.scriptureunion.org.uk/light). This should suggest the idea of giving our concerns to God and of our receiving his provision and care. This image provides the backdrop for the remainder of the service. Alternatively, the previous week a Sunday group could prepare an actual backdrop of this on material or strong paper. You will need volunteers prepared to take part as indicated in the outline below.

No worries!
Introduce 'Mr Worry', who looks suitably worried and careworn. If the character from the *Mr Men* books (Roger Hargreaves) will be familiar to your congregation, make use of this idea. Mr Worry announces to the congregation, 'I'm so worried!'

Ask everyone for suggestions as to what he might be worried about, such as food, fashion, having enough money, job, problems in the world. Each time a suggestion is made, Mr Worry says, 'Yes, I'm worried about…'. Several volunteer helpers write each 'worry' on a box (have an assortment of different shapes and sizes) and put it into a large rucksack on Mr Worry's back. The rucksack begins to bulge and Mr Worry acts as if it's becoming very heavy and gradually sinks to the ground, exhausted.

At this point, thank the volunteer helpers and ask them to return to their seats. Mr Worry stays, slumped under the weight of his bag, at the front – as a reminder about the result of worrying and also ready to participate later in the service.

Ask the congregation: Do you worry about things? Do you ever feel you can't move because of the weight of your worries? In the earlier reading we heard that Jesus said we don't need to worry (Matthew 6:25). Ask the congregation for their ideas about why Jesus said this.

God who cares
Comment that the reading gave some examples of how God cares and provides for his creation (Matthew 6:26–30). But why should we believe this? Where's the evidence?

Ask what examples of God's provision Jesus gave (he feeds the birds; he 'clothes' the landscape with flowers and grass). Comment that we have plenty of other evidence too. Ask for some examples. Indicate the foods and flowers everyone has brought. Ask people to think about all the material provision they see in their lives and the beauty of the world they have witnessed.

Say that we can all probably think of many examples of God's great care. Now invite a volunteer (pre-arranged) to come to the front to share a particular personal story of how they have seen God's care demonstrated in their own life, emphasising the need to trust him.

Trust him
Say that if God is like this, then we can trust him (Matthew 6:30–32). If we stop worrying about things like money, food, clothes, personal success, then we will be able to focus on what's really important – living for God (Matthew 6:33).

Invite Mr Worry to stand again, which he does, staggering as if his bag is very heavy. Point out to everyone how weighed down he is by all his concerns about life. Tell him that if he trusted God for all he needed, he wouldn't need to carry this heavy load. Ask him if he'd like to do that now and he responds affirmatively, several times by saying, 'I'm going to trust God!' Help him take off the heavy bag. Mr Worry celebrates (eg whooping and jumping), then runs through the centre of the congregation cheering. As he exits, encourage everyone to applaud. There is a sense in which this acknowledges Mr Worry's 'performance', but it can also express thankfulness to God for his care for us.

Freed to live for God
Conclude by saying that the challenge for all of us is to trust God with our concerns – not so that we can have an easy life, but so that we are free to get on with wholehearted living for him.

Finish by reading again Matthew 6:31–34.

Prayers of confession

Ask everyone to take the cut-out drawing of open hands which they were given at the start. Ask them to write or draw on the hand anything they are particularly worried about.

Ask them to think about how this anxiety might have got in the way of their trusting God. If they trusted God, would they still have this worry?

Introduce a time of confession. Invite everyone to join in with the response: **Father, forgive us.**

Father, we are sorry for when our own worries get in the way of living for you.
Father, forgive us.
Father, we are sorry for behaving as though what we want is more important than what you want.
Father, forgive us.
Father, we are sorry for when we have not trusted you.
Father, forgive us.
Amen.

Prayers of intercession

Holding on to the thoughts about God's abundant provision, ask everyone, on their cut-out hand shapes, to write the names of or draw anyone they know who is in need – anyone suffering in parts of the world where there is famine, or local needs in your community or church.

Ask everyone to focus on what they've written or drawn on their cut-out hands. Invite everyone to bring these needs to God, trusting in his care. As appropriate, ask them to do this holding out their own hands as an expression of their trust in God and readiness to receive from him.

Arrange in advance for several members of your congregation, of all ages, to lead everyone in prayer: thanking God for his provision, bringing to him needs in the world, local community, your church and personal concerns. After each prayer, encourage the congregation to respond with the words:
Father, we trust you.

Conclude this time by praying together the Lord's Prayer.

Invite everyone to keep their hands shape safe and put it in a place where they will see it often in the coming week. Encourage people to use it as a reminder to:

thank God for all his care for them
trust him for their needs
pray for others in need.

Response

Say that it's great that we can leave our concerns with God because we can trust him to care for us. But this is not just so that we can have a comfortable life. The result of God providing for us is that we can concentrate on living for him. That includes the challenge to show God's care for his creation.

As an expression of your trust in God and to show his love for others, invite everyone to join in one of the following activities:

- Invite people to give money for a particular project known to your church family which will provide for the needs of others. This might be to support a Christian ministry locally or overseas, or a community project. Tell people in advance that there will be this opportunity to give during the service, so that they come prepared. Collect the offerings and bring them to the front. Thank God for his provision and pray that these gifts will be a blessing to those who receive them.

- Announce that during the week you will be distributing the harvest gifts of food and flowers to those in your church community or those known to church members who have various needs. Ask people to sign up at the end of the service if they could be involved in this, giving availability and contact details. You might need to advise people in advance to bring their diaries!

- Before the service, do some research into practical needs in your church family (eg gardening, lawnmowing, shopping, ironing for the elderly, babysitting for busy parents, visiting those on their own). As above, ask people to sign up to take on one of these practical tasks.

Encourage everyone to see this giving of personal time and resources as an expression of their own trust in God and thankfulness for his provision for them.

God's blessing

Explain that you are going to receive God's blessing as you share in a meal together (or simple refreshments), as a reminder of his good provision for all your needs, and the challenge to trust him and live for him.

As an expression of your thankfulness, sing a hymn or song such as:

'Now thank we all our God'
'Praise God from whom all blessings flow'

Then invite people to the area where they will eat together, however light or substantial.

As people enjoy this time together, display again the PowerPoint of images of God's provision (see 'Introduction') and/or the image of hands stretched out towards the onlooker (as described in 'Bible talk'). Encourage people to continue the 'What's my name?' quiz. Give the answers and a prize to the winner.

The Light Range...

Welcome to Scripture Union's family of *Light* resources.
There's a leader's guide, and children's and young people's materials for each age group, plus lots of extra resources to enhance your work with them. For more information visit **www.scriptureunion.org.uk/light**

5s and Under

5-8s

8-11s

11-14s

14-18s

All-age worship

Light for the Lectionary makes the approach and expertise of Scripture Union's market leading *Light* resources available to churches using a lectionary to explore and teach the Bible in their all-age worship services.

LightLive is a new addition to the family of *Light* resources. Register free at **www.lightlive.org** today and discover an exciting approach to children's, youth and all-age ministry.